D1118342

The Fisherman's
TACKLE BOX
𝕭𝖎𝖇𝖑𝖊

To William ...

Don't catch 'em all!

Frank Mains

The Fisherman's
TACKLE BOX
Bible

Frank Davis

PELICAN PUBLISHING COMPANY
Gretna 2003

I wish to thank the people at Pelican Publishing Company, Inc.:
the publisher, Milburn Calhoun, my editor, Nina Kooij,
my typesetter, Talissa Verdine-Esprit, my publicist, Rachel Carner,
and my sales champion, Larry Babin

The word "Pelican" and the depiction of a pelican are trademarks
of Pelican Publishing Company, Inc., and are registered
in the U.S. Patent and Trademark Office.

Library of Congress Cataloging-in-Publication Data

Davis, Frank, 1942-
  The fisherman's tackle box bible / Frank Davis.
    p. cm.
  ISBN 1-58980-128-8 (pbk. : alk. paper)
  1. Fishing—Louisiana. I. Title.
  SH501 .D38 2003
  799.1'09763—dc21

                    2003004249

Printed in the United States of America

Published by Pelican Publishing Company, Inc.
1000 Burmaster Street, Gretna, Louisiana 70053

To Elise, Matthew, Zachary, and Benjamin,
the greatest little grandkids in the whole wide world
and Paw-Paw's real fishing buddies!

Contents

Introduction

I've always loved the old expression that goes, "The fishing is always good . . . but sometimes the catching ain't worth a dang!"

And it's on that very principle and because of its implications that this book was conceived and written. Actually, all the tips and pointers you're about to read I've written before, in hundreds of e-mails, in newspaper columns, and even on the backs of brown paper bags for fishermen I've met in grocery-store checkout lines. But all those other writings obviously didn't direct or teach properly, because it seems that week after week after month after year I keep having to write the same stuff over and over again.

And then I got to thinking. Maybe that's because there were too many sources to go to and too many different things to read—e-mails, paper-bag notes, newspaper columns. Maybe I wasn't making the critical presentation to the masses all at one time. Maybe I needed a book!

So that's what this is—a *book* that contains absolutely nothing other than what you positively need to know in order to *find and catch fish*. No flowery stories. No Ph.D.-level ichthyological dissertation. No mumbo-jumbo. No bull chips. No hype. No gingerbread and filigree. Just facts—the stripped-down facts. Your basic and to-the-point what, when, where, why, and how of catching fish, written in easy-to-understand verbiage.

What you're going to find in these pages are the simple

answers to all the questions that you ever wanted to pose to the so-called fishing experts. In chapter after verse, you will now have "the secrets revealed." This is how the veterans and the guides and the pros fish! These are the methods used by those anglers who have mastered the sport, who possess the cleric mysticism to be able to find fish no matter what the conditions, and who regularly show up on the tote boards at the major rodeos to take home the new cars, boats, motors, and trailers. By using these tactics and techniques, you too will be able to catch your share of those fish!

Of course, I never intended for this book to be relegated to the "Reference Rack" at the public library, stashed away with the collectible Tolstoy and Hemingway in your mahogany-paneled study, or even restricted to coffee-table status with the family Bible. This "bible" was always destined for inclusion in the tackle box, where you could snatch it up in an instant, on the water, in the middle of a fishing trip, and find the answers to any of your fishing questions between the last cast and the next!

I will tell you, though, that reading chapters like a novel (and reading them over and over again) will serve to burn them indelibly into the recesses of your mind, thus making all the tricks seemingly second nature.

And in case you're wondering, the information contained in these pages is not limited to any one particular fishing spot. Data is based primarily on species characteristics, which means that the tactics you use to find trout and reds and flounder are as valid along the coastline of Mississippi and Texas as they are inside the bayous of Southeast Louisiana. And here at home, they apply to fishing Lake Pontchartrain, Hopedale, Cocodrie, Lafitte, Pointe a la Hache, Port Sulphur, Delacroix Island, the Chef, the Rigolets, Golden Meadow, Leeville, Myrtle Grove, Grand Isle, the Fourchon, Venice, and essentially every other popular fishing spot on the coastal map.

So having said all this, may I recommend that you read "the

bible" from cover to cover, not once but several times. Absorb the fishing facts within its chapters as a sponge absorbs water. Then commit the information you glean to memory and recall it at every fishing opportunity. I give you my word that if you do this, all of a sudden you'll begin finding more fish than ever before, catching them a whole lot easier than you did in the past, and realizing a whole new enjoyment of the sport.

The Fisherman's
TACKLE BOX
Bible

CHAPTER 1

As Good as Gospel . . . Just Ask Frank

Every day of my life I get faxes, phone calls, letters, and e-mails, each asking for the answers to a host of fishing questions. They run the gamut from which is the best bait to use for trout at Golden Meadow to which tidal range produces the hottest feeding action in Barataria Bay. In the past, I answered the questions and then tossed out the mail. But when I decided to put this book together, I had a better idea! It only made sense that if one person wanted the answer to a particular question, there must be others looking for that same answer. So in this chapter I'm pleased to include what I call, "As Good as Gospel . . . Just Ask Frank."

Dear Frank: Is it legal to fish in the Industrial Canal in New Orleans? We went out there recently and there were eight boats fishing inside the channel at the second drawbridge.
  Lisa—the fishin' gal

Dear Lisa: It is illegal to fish inside the Industrial Canal because you can actually get run over and killed by barge traffic. The Harbor Police control the Industrial Canal and they are mean motor scooters when you break the law! I don't recommend you get on their bad side.
  You can, however, fish out in the lake, out past the Seabrook. Just stay out of the main channel (for your own safety). Let's you and me agree not to tell everybody about it, though, okay?
  Frank D

Dear Frank: I live in Hammond and would like to bring my granddaughter fishing. I heard about some New Orleans fishing piers you showed on WWL-TV once. The problem is I'm not familiar with where the piers are (I don't get out much).

Would you please give me directions on how to get there?
Reed V

Dear Reed: The television show I did highlighted three piers—one at Bonnabel Boulevard, another at Williams Boulevard, and a third one under the Seabrook Bridge on Lakeshore Drive at the site of the Industrial Canal. All are open to the public with easy access.

To get to Bonnabel, get off either the I-10 or Veterans Highway at Bonnabel. Then go all the way to the lake. The pier is adjacent to the boat launch and sits off to the right when you are facing the launch.

To get to Williams, get off either the I-10 or Veterans Highway at Williams. Then go past the Pontchartrain Center, go over the levee past the floodgates, hang a left at Treasure Chest Casino, and follow the road around to the massive U-shaped pier.

And finally, to get to the Seabrook Pier, which I'm proud to say is also called the Frank Davis Fishing Pier, you need to take Lakeshore Drive on the New Orleans lakefront to the Seabrook Bridge over the Industrial Canal. Then on the west side of the bridge, take a quick dogleg to the right and go under the bridge approach all the way to the canal. The state-of-the-art pier, complete with lights for night fishing and a ramp for handicapped access, sits off to the left under the up-ramp. Just don't fish from the parking lot into the Industrial Canal!
Frank D

Hey, Frank: Is there any way to get tide information in advance? I see it for the current day, but is it posted somewhere for a few days in advance?
Carlton M

Dear Carlton: There are several answers to your question. First, you can check your local map company, bookstore, or nautical shop and buy an annual book of tides. Yep—one really does exist. All you need to do is convert it to our waters. Or . . .

If you're a computer person, you can go to www.rodnreel. com and click on tidal charts. Most of the popular fishing areas in South Louisiana and South Mississippi are posted on that Web site.

Frank D

Frank: On one of my days off recently my wife and I rode by Tite's Place on U.S. Highway 11 at North Shore. Unfortunately we were not able to launch there because my wife was not able to back down the ramp while I handled the boat (she is sort of new at this).

So I am planning on going to Fort Pike or maybe fish the Causeway, using the Bonnabel launch instead. Do you have any thoughts on this?

The next question is—how important is live bait, since neither of these locations sell bait?

Chuck I

Dear Chuck: Launching at Fort Pike or at the Rigolets Harbor Marina definitely is an option. You can also put in at Bonnabel if you're a veteran lake fisherman and you're familiar with the structure around the Causeway.

Live bait could mean the difference between catching fish and having to stop on the way home for a bucket of chicken. And you're right—there is never any live shrimp available at Fort Pike. However, if you go just across the Rigolets Bridge to the Rigolets Harbor Marina you'll usually find all the live bait you want. At Bonnabel, though, there's no live bait around for miles!

Frank D

Hey, Frank: Could you please describe for me how to tie a Carolina rig? It's all I hear about lately. And can you also recommend the right knot to use when tying on the Carolina? I certainly would be grateful.

Emmett H

Dear Emmett: Follow carefully: Take the end of the monofilament or braided line as it comes off your rod tip, after passing through the rod guides, and thread it though the hole in a quarter-ounce (or slightly heavier) egg sinker. Then thread the line through a small red plastic bead. Next tie the end of the line to one side of a barrel swivel. You're half-finished!

Now make a 14-inch to 18-inch leader, preferably of 30-pound-test monofilament, and tie a 2/0 Kahle hook to one end. Then take the other end and tie it onto the opposite side of the barrel swivel you attached to the mono coming off the rod.

That, Emmett, is a Carolina rig, otherwise known as a sliding sinker rig. And the best knots to use when rigging it are either the Double Overhand Improved Clinch or the Palomar. I personally prefer the Palomar!

All in all, the Carolina rig is probably one of the best bottom-fishing rigs ever devised and is just what you need when fishing for trout, reds, and flounder.

Frank D

Dear Frank: Where can I go with my family to catch some crabs and what time of night or day is best to catch big blue crabs? Also, I prefer to stay in the N'Awlins area. Need some serious help!

VTM

Dear VTM: Just about all the fishing hotspots are also crabbing hotspots. That would be any of the connecting bayous and canals at the Rigolets, Bayou Sauvage at the Chef, Bayou Liberty where it meets Lake Pontchartrain, Lake Pontchartrain at the New Orleans Lakefront Airport, all along the Highway

11 bridge, the North Shore and South Shore shoreline, Irish Bayou—the list goes on and on.

Now, if you ever do decide to leave the N'Awlins environ, just remember that any deep channel anywhere in the marsh where you find good clean water is usually a prime crabbing spot, especially for the round-net fisherman. Of course, if you want to try crabbing from the bank, that's a whole other story. I suggest you make a phone call to my office at 504-529-6431 and get a current list of the "really productive" bank-fishing spots. It'll put you light-years ahead of the game. Just talk with Gail Guidry.

When's the best time to go crabbing? That's an easy answer—it's whenever you can go!

Frank D

Dear Frank: I was talking to some old-timers a while back and they told about a very deep hole at Chef Menteur Pass called "the Minutes." They kept saying it's about 90 feet deep. They also said this is where they used to catch tarpon. Is this an old wives' tale or what?

Craig B

Dear Craig: "The Minutes" does actually exist, and not only was it a great spot for catching tarpon in the heyday of tarpon fishing in Lake Pontchartrain, it was always—and still is!—a good spot to catch drums, sheepshead, croakers, gafftops, redfish, and a bunch of other species.

It's located in Chef Pass at the biggest curve and it got its name because the water there is so deep fishermen used to say it takes "a couple of minutes" for your bait to reach the bottom. Actually, the reason for the depth is the location of the almost 90-degree curve in the pass. As the tide goes in and out, the force of the moving water eats away at the bottom, making it deeper and deeper over the years. So the next time you're out fishing at the Chef, make a stop at "the Minutes." But bring a lot of anchor rope!

Frank D

Dear Frank: I just moved to New Orleans from California. I have done most of my fishing in the Pacific. My question is where can I find beginners' information for fishing in the area? I don't have a boat, but spend some time on Lake Pontchartrain once in a while. Where are the best places to go on this lake and what kind of fish are all the fishermen catching?

Patrick M

Dear Patrick: Congratulations on your decision to join us here in God's Country. Rest assured I'll do whatever I can to help you learn to fish here. First thing I recommend you do is religiously visit www.rodnreel.com. It's a pretty decent page concerned with fishing in Southeast Louisiana. Once you get past all the whiny ol' men, the rest of the information is pretty decent. Then pick up a copy of *Louisiana Outdoors* every month and read it religiously from cover to cover. It's one of the most informative publications we have here in the state.

Then I suggest you watch my TV shows every Thursday night and Friday morning on WWL-Channel 4. I'll keep you abreast of all the latest catches, where they're coming from, and what baits are producing. The segment is called "The Fishin' Game Report."

And you can read this book several times from cover to cover. Then if you find you still have unanswered questions, you can memorize my e-mail address (frankd@frankdavis.com) so that you can direct all your specific questions to me personally.

Frank D

Dear Frank: How does one go about putting a crab on a hook? I talked to this guy in the barbershop a while back and he told me that they were catching some pretty big redfish on crabs. He said the smallest one that they had caught was 29 inches! I have never used crabs for bait before, so I'm not really sure how to properly put a crab on a hook. Any info that you can give would be very much appreciated.

Aaron W

Dear Aaron: The old saying is, "A redfish would cross a busy interstate highway at drive-time to get to a crab." And over the years, after fishing reds with cracked crab, I've become convinced of that. So here's how it's done. You first remove the crab's top shell and discard it as chum. Then you crack it into a right half and a left half. Then you divide it again. If you've done this right, you should end up with four crab "quarters."

Now you tie on a Carolina rig (sliding sinker, swivel, shock leader about 14 inches long, and a Kahle hook on the end) and simply run the hook right through the middle of the crab quarter, exposing the barb. Then make your cast and let the bait sit on the bottom. If there are redfish (or drums) around, it won't be long before they pick up the bait and attempt to swim away. All you do is set the hook.

Just one variation here, though. The bigger the redfish you're after, the bigger the chunk of crab should be. For those 29-inch reds you mentioned, I'd entice them with an entire half of a crab; and for 36-inch bull reds, go with the whole thing! I recommend that when you hook on a half or whole crab, you run the hook through the back fin swimmer instead of through the shell—this makes it easier for the barb to produce a better hook-set. Oh, yeah—and check your bait often. Little hardheads and pinfish can strip out the crabmeat from the shell like a pack of piranha.

Frank D

Yo, Frank: Got a question! What's the secret to keeping live shrimp alive for a long time? I have a bubble pump. Any other tips?

Wallace E

Dear Wally: A couple of suggestions. First, make sure you have a good airstone on the end of your bubble pump. You can get these at any pet store and they break down the bubbles into ultrafine oxygen that is more easily dissolved in the water in your live well.

Next, be sure you don't overcrowd the shrimp—they need space. If you pile them into a live well or a white bucket like cross-packed sardines, nothing you can do will keep them alive but for a few minutes.

And finally, the next time you're at your favorite sporting-goods store, pick up a pack of "Bait-Saver." It comes in both granular form and tablets and is quite effective in prolonging the life of live bait, especially live croakers, Cocahoes, and shiners, by eliminating urea from the water.

Frank D

Dear Mr. Frank: We just moved to Abita Springs. And I would like to take my six-year-old fishing. We have a 15-foot canoe. The problem is I don't know a lot about fishing or where we could go close by. I was hoping that you could help.

Toby J

Dear Toby: Up in your neck of the woods you have the Amite, the Comite, the Bogue Chitto, the Pearl, and a bunch of other small rivers you could try (you want to be sure to stay on *small rivers* with a canoe and a six-year-old!).

What I recommend you do is locate all the bait shops in your area. Then visit them on a regular basis, get in tight with some of the local anglers, and start picking some brains. Find out who fishes where with what and what they catch, how to get there, where to launch, and so forth. Nobody knows fishin' better than the locals!

Also be sure to get a Standard Mapping Company "Photo-Map" of the area in which you live and start studying it. In fact, memorize it! Remember, before you can make a gumbo you gotta be a master at making the roux!

Frank D

Dear Frank: I need help. I am trying to learn more about fishing and watching the tides. I like to fish the Causeway Bridge but cannot find a tide table to help. Do you know what the difference is at the Causeway Bridge versus the I-10 Bridge?

Jim M

Dear Jim: You don't need a book, just a formula. Whatever the Grand Isle tide is on the nightly weather report, you add 3 hours and 40 minutes to it to get the Causeway high tide, and subtract 3 hours and 40 minutes from it to get Causeway low tide. Of course, all this goes right out the window if the wind is blowing 15 miles per hour or better against the tide!

Frank D

Dear Frank: I was wondering if you could please give me some information on fishing in Chef Menteur Pass. Do you know if it is still a good place to fish at? If so, where are the best places?

Thank you.

Kevin C

Kevin: The Chef, like the Rigolets, remains a very good place to fish, especially for trout, reds, and flounder. All the old traditional hotspots—the bridge stanchions, the Hospital Wall, the Minutes, Big Cedar and Little Cedar bayous, the Marquis Canal—still produce fish under good conditions (good tide and clean water).

Like everywhere else in the Pontchartrain/Borgne estuary, live shrimp and live Cocahoes work best during "live bait" season; artificials can be used after you first find the fish with live bait. You will have to do a little scouting and moving to get on the fish and to stay with them.

But would I try the Chef? You betcha!

Frank D

Hi, Frank: I don't feel like driving to Shell Beach for my next fishing trip. Shouldn't the fish be in the same sort of spots around Bayou Bienvenue?

I also never could find the "Bulk Plant." Can you give me an idea where it is?

Where else do you suggest besides the "Hot Water Canal"? I always get hung up on the riprap, and it's like a parade of boats through there. The story is the same at the "locks." Any help will be greatly appreciated.

Sandra

Dear Sandra: I mean, it's not like Shell Beach is off on the other side of the galaxy, for God sakes! And if you really want to get into fish at certain times of the year, I heartily suggest you opt for "the beach" over Bienvenue (because no—just because they're active at Shell Beach doesn't mean they're going to be active at Bienvenue). That's the biology of it all!

You can't miss the Bulk Plant. Find the Hot Water Canal and the Michoud Slip, then go upstream a skosh, and there's the Bulk Plant smack-dab in front of you. Keep in mind, though, that all three of these places are summer haunts and may not be that productive during cold weather.

As far as avoiding the riprap, that's why God made chugging and popping corks! Keep the bait suspended off the bottom and you won't get so hung up. And finally, when you no longer see the parade of boats that you're complaining about, the fish will have gone!

Frank D

Frank: I live in Covington and do not have a boat. Are there any good fishing spots from the shoreline that are close by?

I have fished the canals at Lacombe and Madisonville but never have any luck. I have heard stories of people catching fish and crabs there, but I guess I am using the wrong bait or doing something wrong. If you could give me any tips or a list of other places to fish, I would certainly appreciate it.

Also do you know of any freshwater spots I can fish from the shoreline that are close by?

Darren A

Darren: Those spots you're fishing are probably just as good as any others you could try.

You got to remember that fishing from the bank is always very difficult and few people ever catch anything at all. The reason is because of circumstance and condition—low water, high water, dirty water, cold water, no bait, too much garbage tossed overboard, and—the *main reason*—too much fishing pressure! Too many people know where all these bank-fishing spots are, so while they're nice spots to fish *from*, they're low on the potential pole for *catching* anything.

So the best I can tell you is just hang in there—the fishing will always be good, but the catching will pretty much suck.

Frank D

Hey Frank: I know that you are the person I need to speak to about this. Can you please tell me how to rig a sliding cork? I am told that it is the only rig to use for catching "big" trout that hang "suspended" right in the middle between the top and the bottom.

Daryl B

Dear Daryl: You're right—the purpose of a sliding cork is to keep the bait suspended at one particular strike depth, cast after cast, without having the hassle of having to pitch a six-foot leader against the wind. Now, I could attempt to tell you that you first slide the monofilament through a red plastic bead, then run the mono through the sliding cork, then position a "bobber stop" above the cork and bead where you want the line to stop "sliding" out, then tie on the appropriate split-shot weight and finally a Kahle hook at the terminal end. But I'm thinking you probably would never envision that in your mind's eye.

So do this—go to your favorite sporting-goods store and

buy a couple of sliding corks and a couple packs of bobber stops (these are the little gizmos that attach to your line to prevent the cork from sliding past 'em). Then all you do is simply follow the very detailed line art on the back of the packaging that shows you exactly how to do it.

It's what I do!

Frank D

Frank: I only have a 17-foot aluminum boat. It can't take rough water. Is the lake my best bet? The trestle always seems to be choppy for small boats. Would I find fishing better at Shell Beach, Hopedale, or Delacroix?

I live on the North Shore near Covington. Also, since I've been out fishing several times with Capt. Phil Robichaux, I would rather fish like him and not use live bait. But every time I see you on TV you are using live bait. Am I wasting my time with artificials?

And last but not least, from what mile marker or visual marker do I start fishing the lake? Are there hotspots to focus on? Are there places in the lake that are not out in the open that are good to fish?

Charles M

Dear Charlie: You can use your 17-foot aluminum boat in the lake at the trestle, but you got to pick your days. On choppy days, stay in port. When the lake lies down, head on out to the trestle, the old Highway 11 Bridge, or the Twin Spans.

Hopedale, Shell Beach, and Delacroix Island are all outstanding spots for small-boat fishermen to try because, as you suggest, these places are protected from the weather and gusty winds. So if you don't mind towing a trailer, try not only the lake but these other "hotspots" as well.

Now, as for the artificial lures, if you want to really perfect the plastic-bait finesse and technique that Phil has mastered over all his years of fishing . . . then go for it!

I, however, have never reached Phil's pinnacle of plastic perfection, so I am forever compelled to bring along on every trip I make artificials as well as market shrimp *and* live bait. In other words, you do whatcha gotta do!

Finally, always start fishing the trestle at Railroad Marker 176. Then move up and down the structure from North Shore to South Shore until you locate the biggest concentrations of fish. When you find them, ease the anchor over and catch yo'sef a mess of 'em!

Frank D

Dear Frank: We just moved here from above the Mason-Dixon line. I would like to know where my family and I could go to do some freshwater bank fishing in this area.

Thank you,

T. Kerns

Mr. Kerns: Southeast Louisiana is not one of those big fishing-freshwater-from-the-bank areas. We've got lots of saltwater fishing from the bank, but freshwater isn't all that prominent.

Some of the more popular spots around, nevertheless, are Bayou Segnette at the park site, Pearl River at both Davis Landing and Crawford's Landing, City Park in New Orleans (there are about seven miles of bream- and bass-producing freshwater canals scattered throughout the park), and the piers and parking areas inside of the Bayou Sauvage National Wildlife Refuge, especially those off U.S. Highway 11 near Irish Bayou.

What you do is use the very same techniques, tactics, and tackle you usta use on the other side of the Mason-Dixon line. Freshwater fishing is still freshwater fishing wherever you go. Best baits are either little white, blue, or yellow tube jigs (or live worms and crickets on a small cork) for bream, and either topwater plugs or black and purple worms Texas rigged with a bullet weight for bass.

Give yourself enough time to scout out each one of these spots, then when you find the fish, don't tell a soul where you found them (except, of course, for me).

Frank D

Hey, Frank: What is the best way you think I should bait my hook with live shrimp? I seem to lose a lot of bait because I'm not hooking them right.

Thanks,

Lori J

Dear Lori: There are two methods considered by most veteran fishermen to be most effective—*headhook and tailhook.*

To headhook, hold the shrimp in your hand so that the head is between your thumb and forefinger. You will notice several black spots inside the head, but you will also notice a somewhat clear area between the black spots. That clear area is where you should run the hook, through and through, from left to right, with your other hand. Most fishermen use this hooking method when fishing a Carolina rig on the bottom.

To tailhook, hold the tail of the shrimp between your thumb and forefinger. Then place the hook through the second to last segment in the shrimp's tail. Many fishermen prefer this hooking method when fishing under a popping or chugging cork. (Personally, regardless of whether I'm fishing top or bottom, I prefer to headhook.)

Frank D

Mr. Frank: I've been fishing the Hopedale and Shell Beach area for a few months and haven't hit the fish really good yet. I don't get to go that often, since I am a medical student, and I don't have enough money for a guide. I was wondering, when you fish in Bayou Guyago, do you fish the ponds and fingers directly off of the bayou? What about fishing points in this area? And do you ever fish inside Guyago at all? Any suggestions would be much appreciated.

John A

Dear John: Yes, I often fish directly in Bayou Guyago, but keep in mind that on some days you have to fish long stretches of it to get anything to happen. Usually, though, the stretches I like to cover (get yourself a quality map of the area and study it until you commit the topography to memory) encompass fishing at the intersections of the bayous, points, ponds, and fingers to which you allude. You will generally find fish at most of these intersections.

Scientifically, that's the correct method to use when working a complex waterway such as Bayou Guyago. You start off in the straightaways; then you pick out intersections where Guyago and other bayous or trainaisses or drains cross each other; then you ease up into the adjoining lagoons and work both the shorelines and the middle ground. And wherever you fish, remember to try the top, the bottom, the deep, and the shallow—first with live bait, then with artificials. And when nothing happens in one spot, you move until you find a spot where it does.

Frank D

Dear Frank: I watched one of your TV shows when you were fishing bull reds at Cocodrie. You kept saying that we should use cracked crab. What's the best way to rig cracked crab? And what size leader, hook, and swivel should I use?

Cyrus B

Dear Cyrus,

For superbig bull reds (those guys over 30 inches long), you want to use a whole crab. For bulls in the 25-inch range, you can get by with a half-crab. For smaller reds, 16 to 24 inches, sometimes even a quarter-crab is all it takes. So first take the top shell off, then crack the crab either in halves or quarters.

Then using a 40-pound-test Carolina rig about 20 inches long, with a heavy-duty barrel swivel, an egg sinker heavy enough to keep the rig on the bottom (could take 1 ounce, could take 3), and a 6/0 Kahle hook tied on with a Palomar knot, run the barb of the hook from the back side to the front side of the crab so that the barb comes all the way through.

On half- and whole crabs, run the hook through the large back swimmeret; on quarter-crabs, simply perforate the center of the crab shell. All that's left is to cast the baited rig out onto a sandbar or shell reef, let it settle to the bottom, and hold on!

Frank D

Dear Frank: How do you boil shrimp so that the shell does not stick like glue to the meat? Every time I boil shrimp, it takes me five minutes to peel a single shrimp!

Michael M

Dear Mike: Very, very simple answer. *Stop overcooking them!* The shells will stick only when you overcook the shrimp (same thing applies to your crawfish).

Here's what you do:

Bring the water to a boil. Season it with salt, pepper, onions, garlic, celery, lemon, seafood boil, and bay leaves. Then drop in the shrimp.

The water will stop boiling. When it comes back to a boil, time the shrimp for exactly 1 minute! Then turn the fire off, take the pot off the burner, drop a half-bag of ice into the boil, put the lid on the pot, and let the shrimp soak for 20 minutes to pick up all of the flavorings.

Now they'll peel like bananas!

Frank D

Dear Frank: Some time back on your television show you showed us a special kind of fish scaler—you even said it was one of the best ones you had ever used. What is the name of it and where can I find one?

Chris

Dear Chris: The name of the fish scaler is "Bicco." It was designed a long time ago by a New Orleanian and is still on the market. It fits your hand beautifully (whether you're right-handed or left-handed), has an indented spot for your thumb to rest, and, because it's made of molded plastic, has a set of serrated scaling points that makes fish cleaning a breeze!

The last ones I bought I got from sporting-goods stores in both Chalmette and Slidell, but no matter where you live you can go to www.google.com, type in Bicco Fish Scaler, and it will take you to a Web site that supplies them. I suggest you buy one for home and another one for your tackle box.

Frank D

Mr. Frank: There was someone that you once suggested the public contact in the Gulf Coast area regarding questions about seafood. Can you tell me the name of the person and how to contact her?

Thank you.

C. Holman

Dear Mr. Holman: The agency is called the Louisiana Seafood Promotion and Marketing Board and the person to talk with is Tracy Mitchell. The number is listed with Directory Assistance under the Louisiana Department of Wildlife and Fisheries. She is the authoritative source for anything having to do with finfish, shellfish, and every other form of food from our Southern seas.

Frank D

Hey, Frank: I seem to remember an article you did once about seasoning a new Dutch oven or black iron pot. Something to do with bacon drippings and baking it in the oven. Since the old black pot is such an important part of cooking Cajun, can you refresh my memory on this procedure? Or can you point me in the right direction? My taste buds thank you in advance.

Phil S

Dear Phil: On pages 13 and 14 of *The Frank Davis Seafood Notebook* cookbook, one of my other bestsellers, there are step-by-step instructions on seasoning your black pot as well as other cast-iron utensils. If you don't have a copy of this book, you really should have one! The explanation is detailed and takes you through the entire step-by-step process. It would be redundant to cover it here, but if you're desperate and need help in the interim, you can also e-mail Gail Guidry at gguidry@wwltv.com and ask her to send you a printout of those pages. She's my assistant and you can tell her I approved it for you.

Frank D

CHAPTER 2

Those Outdoor Outtakes

The average viewer or listener hardly ever gets to see or hear them! That's because every on-air TV talent directs their editors to waste no time "scrubbing" the videotape to edit them out, and radio hosts quickly bleep them out of existence with their seven-second-delay button. So it's only in reading chapters like this one that you get to sneak a peek and appreciate the real story behind "Those Outdoor Outtakes."

HOOKED IN THE NOSE—BARB AND ALL

So here we were, my guide Phil Robichaux, my cameraman Terry Jones, and myself, following this massive school of big redfish down the shoreline of Bay Round near Lafitte. And the excitement among the three of us was at a fever pitch.

"Look, look! Straight ahead of us! They're going around the point! Throw out in front of them!" Phil shouted to us, casting and backcasting as quickly as he could in an almost rapid-fire mechanical rhythm.

And that's when it happened!

On the verge of frustration, having gotten no strike following his last cast and about to see the school swim out of range, Phil reeled in the quarter-ounce jig head, fitted with the H&H tuxedo-color Cocahoe tail, whipped the bait instinctively behind him in the backcast as hard as he could, and slung it immediately forward with every strand of muscle in his arm and shoulder.

"Aaarrrggghhh!" The shriek was bloodcurdling.

All those years I had shot the fishing-show episodes and numerous other television assignments with Terry Jones, I had never heard him make that sound. And what was ironic was he seemed to bellow it out right about the same time that Phil yelled out, "Aw man, look at this backlash! What did I snag?"

"Don't pull! Don't pull!" Terry screeched, holding his face in his hands as if he were going to sneeze. And that's when Phil and I both realized what had happened. Terry had been caught—in the fleshy part of the nose that forms the left nostril.

"You're what I snagged?" Phil asked Terry.

"Uh-huh," Terry grunted with his mouth open, his body hunched over about 30 degrees, arms separated and poised in a position similar to a Catholic priest blessing the bread and wine during the offertory.

"You're hooked in the nose, Terry?" I asked in disbelief.

"Uh-huh!" He nodded, the flexible plastic Cocahoe tail vibrating with every affirmative shake of his head. Then he made that noise again.

I rushed over, hoping that my medical training in the army would allow me to remember how to painlessly extract a sharp object from human soft tissue. All I could see, though, was the body of the jig head past the bend in the hook and the plastic tail dangling from Terry's nose.

"Whew! The barb and everything is in there, Terry."

"Get it out!" That's all he kept saying over and over. But he never said it in a cry of desperation. It was more like a line out of a Three Stooges movie.

Now I think it's important that I take a moment to explain what Phil was doing during this moment of tragedy. First, with a quick glance, he instantaneously evaluated Terry's overall condition. He observed that the imbedded hook was preventing any bleeding, which immediately disqualified Terry from being a candidate who needed to be rushed by ambulance to the nearest hospital with an intensive care unit. Secondly, using his finest bedside manner, he leaned slightly toward Terry and somewhat sympathetically asked, "Ya okay?"

Terry made that sound once more and nodded positively again, the Cocahoe shivering spasmodically in his nostril as he maintained his priestly pose. I couldn't help but wonder in distraction what it would take to duplicate that kind of action on the lure as I retrieved it through the water. But my ponderings were shattered by Terry, who resumed screaming something about "taking it out!"

And that's when Phil decided once and for all that his old buddy would be fine. So immediately he pulled off some line to give his snagged hook some slack, dropped the rod and reel still attached to the bait that was still attached to Terry's nose into the bottom of the boat, picked up another rod and reel, kicked the trolling motor back into high bypass, and continued pursuing and casting for the school of redfish that made its way down the shoreline.

"C'mon, Frank, Terry's fine. We'll get that hook out in a minute! Start casting. The reds are getting away!"

True story.

Note: Using talents I mastered as a medic in the army, I did manage to get the hook (which, incidentally, was buried pretty deep) out of Terry's nose with very little pain. My cameraman does carry a scar, but from that day forward he no longer fishes behind Phil Robichaux (or anywhere within range of his notorious backcast)!

HONEY, JUST HOLD THE ROPE!

I have a passion for hanging out at boat ramps, especially the back-down kind, just to watch the parade of proficiency when it comes to the recreational process known as "launching." D'ja ever watch that? It's hilarious!

The best episode took place one morning at Crawford's Landing on Pearl River, just as the sun was peeking up over the horizon. Some guy in an old Chevy pickup truck, towing a big, brand-new bass boat, pulled up to the back-down ramp and jumped out. His wife, riding shotgun, got out on the passenger side of the vehicle.

The driver immediately began lecturing the woman in a demeaning way, saying, "Now you don't have to do anything technical—nothing hard. All I want you to do is hold the rope for me while I back her in! Don't direct me, don't give me driving instructions, don't even offer me any suggestions. All you got to do is hold the rope, okay? Nothing more! Got that? Think you can do that?"

The woman receiving the onslaught merely shook her head in disbelief and said nothing in response. She walked up to the boat, took hold of the terminal end of the bow line, and held it tightly as her hubby began backing the rig down into the water.

When the transom rose up and began floating, the fisherman behind the wheel popped the truck transmission in low, lurched forward, slid the trailer out from under the buoyant bass rig, and headed for the parking area.

His aide, his wife "the deckhand," the lady with the rope, just stood there doing what she was told—holding the rope! All of a sudden, everybody standing around the ramp—the other boaters who were waiting to launch their rigs, all the attendants—started to laugh uproariously.

It seems the rope, which obviously had never been tied to the boat, had pulled free from the bow when the driver backed the boat off the trailer. So there was this luxurious bass rig, floating down the river in the current. And on the shore, there was this gentle quiet lady, holding the end of a rope, watching the boat drift away.

"Why in hell didn't you run and grab the boat?" the driver screamed at the top of his lungs.

Confidently, in a voice soft-spoken, the lady on the dock looked her companion squarely in the eyes and said, "You told me very specifically that all you wanted me to do was hold the rope. *Well, I'm holding the rope!*"

Note: I think it would be safe to assume that this couple

doesn't fish together anymore. And would you really be surprised if I told you that that decision was made by the wife?

MAC'S SNAKE AMONG THE DECOYS

Back in the late sixties and early seventies, the Chateau Charles Hotel in Lake Charles every year invited members of the *Louisiana Conservationist* magazine staff for opening weekend of duck season. The late McFadden Duffy, who was magazine editor at the time, Bob Dennie, the assistant editor, and myself, who had joined the team as the magazine's outdoor feature writer, would all pack up our shotguns and shells, shut down the Wildlife and Fisheries office on Royal Street, and head west to mix a little business with pleasure.

The way the hunt worked was we would meet bright and early in the morning at about 3:15 in the hotel dining room, have breakfast with the rest of the invited media, catch a hotel shuttle to the boat launch, load the gear in our respective two-man pirogues, and paddle down the bayou in "convoy" to the sunken blinds on the Southwest Louisiana marsh.

This one particular year, Mac had been teamed up with some guy name Zeke, who worked as the new outdoors editor for a small newspaper near Tallulah. Zeke had concocted this plan where he would go to the launch the night before, load up his and Mac's decoys and shell buckets and paddles, cover them with a tarp to protect them from the overnight dew, and then use the pre-prep as a means to sleep later than the rest of us in the morning. Zeke later admitted that while Mac had decided to meet the others at breakfast, Zeke's plan was to skip morning eggs and grits and bacon, drive to the landing in just enough time to be there when the rest of the crew arrived, take his shotgun and box of shells out of the trunk of his car, rendezvous with Mac, step into the boat, and head off—*well rested*—on the morning hunt.

And the plan might have worked too, except for one little technicality!

Shortly before five in the morning, Zeke came storming up

the road to the launch. All the other hunters were already there, loading pirogues with decoys, Labrador retrievers, personal gear bags, bug dope, flashlights, extra ponchos, and all the other items duck hunters take along with them on their daily waterfowl jaunts.

"Hey, you guys should have done like me and Mac," Zeke teased them. "I stashed all our stuff in the pirogue last night— no heavy work this morning. Just get in the boat and zoop— we're on our way!"

He stepped into the pirogue with his side-by-side Savage 12-gauge wedged under his right armpit, dropped two No. 6s in the chambers, and pushed the safety slide over the triggers. "C'mon, Mr. Duffy!" he jokingly shouted to Mac, who was talking to several writers at the shuttle bus. "The boat's leaving, pod'nuh, and we got ducks to hunt!"

Now the rest of this story is subject to variable narration, depending upon who tells it. But most of us do concede that thankfully the pirogue had not drifted too far off the mud bank and into the center of the bayou when the obvious happened.

Suddenly there was a rustling noise that appeared to emanate from under the tarpaulin in the bow of the pirogue. Zeke later told us he could even hear the decoys clanking together. Initially facing the bank, still hassling Mac, Zeke quickly turned when he heard the sound, bent slightly forward, and strained to see what was in the boat. Even in the dim glow of the single mercury vapor lamp on the boat-ramp light pole, Zeke made no mistake identifying the form of the big brown snake that was quickly slithering toward him.

Instinct (and fear) must have taken over! Because the startled small-town journalist suddenly spun around toward the bow, assumed a Rambo split-legged stance, pushed aside the safety, lowered the barrels, and—*from the hip*—loosed both chambers on the snake . . . *as well as the plywood bottom of his pirogue!*

They say that total surprise sometimes keeps persons who observe a tragedy from reacting appropriately. And that must certainly have been what happened to the 20 or so of us who saw the mishap occur in that predawn fog. Because not a one of us—especially Mac Duffy—rushed over to Zeke to lend him a hand as he slowly sank to his neck in the frigid Lake Charles bayou. It was either that or the fact that we had all fallen down on the ground and were laughing so hard we just didn't hear his plaintive, frosty pleas for help!

I know he didn't drown that morning, but I also don't remember Zeke ever hunting with us again.

ZARA SPOOK BACKCAST TO THE CROTCH

You know what a Zara Spook looks like, right? A kinda cigar-shaped hard-plastic floating lure fitted with two sets of dangerous sharp-pointed treble hooks. Anyone will tell you they're dynamite for fishing speckled trout on the surface!

Well, that's what we were using them for as I fished out of Golden Meadow early one summer morning with my old friend Capt. John Aucoin and my cameraman-in-those-days, Terry Jones. On anchor near one of the broken islands in the Timbalier chain, we had pummeled the shallows with the bait for about an hour. Virtually every time the lure made contact with the water, a trout exploded on it! So before long, we could cast for the big fish nearly on autopilot.

And that's when misfortune always happens!

With John casting off the bow, Terry throwing from near the center console, and me whipping baits off the stern, Zara Spooks were buzzing around our heads like gnats on a windless day.

"I guess we had better watch our backcasts!" Terry cautioned both John and me. But before I could decipher exactly what he had said, I suddenly felt this stinging pain in my crotch, high on the right side of my thigh!

"Oh—I bet that hurts!" John moaned.

"Hey, Frank," Terry advised laughingly, "I don't think I would tug on the line if I were you!"

Unfortunately, though, only John and Terry could see the

position of the topwater lure. I couldn't see it from the front nor from behind. In fact, I needed a mirror to see it at all. And reaching it was totally out of the question. But it was there! And it was imbedded! I had backcast it such that the whipping action of the monofilament buried the treble hooks smack dab between my legs in the center of my crotch.

"Okay, you guys," I pleaded, "one of y'all take some pointy-nose pliers and get me loose, okay?"

There was no response. Instead, John and Terry just kept fishing.

"Hey—y'all gonna help me here or what?" I repeated my request. Still nothing! They just gingerly glanced over, bending forward slightly to get a better view, to see that in fact the hooks were where they suspected they were.

"Uh-uh, bruh!" John laughed. "I ain't squatting down there and probing around with no pliers! You never can tell who's watching you out here with a pair of binoculars, and from far off you can't see that Zara Spook!"

"Yeah, Frank," Terry chimed in, smiling and shaking his head in refusal. "You're on your own with this one!"

Looking back, I truly hope no one *was* watching that day with binoculars. I promise you I would have been awfully embarrassed if I knew someone was watching a full-grown man, sitting at the stern of the boat with his pants down around his thighs, probing and prying strangely with a pair of pliers in a most unusual place.

So what's the moral of this story? The moral is . . . camaraderie aside, there are just some things testosterone won't allow your fishing buddies to do!

CHAPTER 3

Perchjerkin' and Panfryin'

They cluster all along the bank under overhanging branches; they pile one on top of the other over hollowed-out gravel beds jutting off points; they stack right at the edge of big lily-pad rafts, where they dart in and out of the root system to snack on passing morsels. Call 'em panfish, sunfish, brim, or bream—once they're coated in cornmeal and they hit the platter, they become the perfect reasons for "Perchjerkin' and Panfryin'."

Well, you can just about figure out that every early February through mid-April is prime time to get out and catch yo'self a whole passel of perch!

So in this chapter I'll share with you the secret as to how you can zero in on your bluegills, your red-ears (which in Southeast Louisiana we like to call your lakerunners), your punkinseeds, your red-bellies, your chinquapins, Lord!—there must be 437,392 different species of perch (well, okay, maybe not that many—but there's a bunch!). And catching them is as easy as stepping in a cow pie in an overcrowded pasture!

USING NATURAL BAITS

It makes no difference what kind of perch you're after or where you head out after them. You can usually bring home a "mess" with nothing more than a box of red worms, a cage full of crickets, or a tub of nightcrawlers. Sure, some folks will tell you that Catalpa worms work best, but I've always found that

41

the old-fashioned baits Paw-Paw usta use seem to come through for me when rooting out bream.

THE ARTIFICIAL TICKET

Of course, there are some anglers who just refuse to catch any kind of fish on anything but artificial bait. Fortunately, God usually feels sorry for this bunch and at times will allow his little fishes to snap at, say, a teeny-weeny plastic grub, or even a feather that's been glued to an itsy-bitsy hook to resemble something that these spunky little fish like to eat. (I can tell you this: The ones that sometimes fall victim to plastic seem to succumb to the little tube-jig types in either black and chartreuse, pearl with blue streamers on the tail, or solid yellow through and through.)

THE FISHING METHODOLOGY

The most common way to catch perch (along with the occasional goggle-eye, which isn't a perch but who cares!) is to fish under a little red and white plastic float. Ideally, you want to suspend the bait—*either natural or artificial*—at the level in the water column where most of the fish seem to be suspending. What that means in very unscientific language is "you want to float the bait somewhere between the top and the bottom at the exact depth where most of the fish are swimming." And unless you were dropped off the roof of a barn onto your head at a very young age, you will quickly be able to figure out how deep to fish once you find the fish.

The other method for catchin' a mess o' perch is tightline fishing. This is where you bait up a little Number 12 hook, or tie on a 1/64th-ounce jig head rigged with one of dem clear grubby-looking things, and cast it out. Then you let it sink to the bottom, and with a series of quick, short twitches you retrieve the lure. The trick is to find out whether the perch want the bait fished slow, fast, close to the bottom, or up near the top. No particular pattern is etched in the biology—you just try a bunch of ways until you hit on one that works. You didn't expect a mathematical formula, did you?

PERCHIN' TACKLE

In the good ol' days, Paw-Paw caught just about every panfish God hatched out using nothing but a cane pole. He'd take one of those 14-footers or such, tie about 15 feet of line onto the whippy tip, knot on a hook, snap on an old wine-bottle cork, bait up with a worm, and sling it out on the gravel bed at his "secret spot in the river." An hour later he'd make his way back to the rickety wharf at the camp with a boatload of bream, all about the size of your right hand. Fortunately, some folks still use Paw-Paw's technique to this day. You can find all the rigging you need for cane polin' at many sporting-goods stores.

But if'n you decide not to cane pole for perch, you most certainly will need some ultralight spinning tackle. Either open-face or spin-cast gear will do, but the lighter the line the better (I usually suggest 4 to 8 pound test). Decide upon natural bait or artificial lures, choose one of those "classic, textbook bream beds," very quietly sneak up to it, and begin pitching! If you choose properly, you should be putting fish in the boat within minutes.

THOSE CLASSIC, TEXTBOOK BREAM BEDS

Freshwater bayous, ponds, sloughs, rivers, canals, and creeks; under bridges, branches, stumps, wharves, docks, boathouses, and duck blinds; over mudflats, gravel pits, shell banks, and under grass rafts—all these places and dozens more will produce bream *if the spots provide both food and cover.* If they hold "feed" and if the little fish can "hide" from the bigger fish, they'll be at those spots and you will catch 'em.

A REAL BATTLE ON YOUR HANDS!

Aren't bream "kids' fish"? Aren't perch for roadside fishermen? Aren't they just a putz-around species? Who told you all that?

Pound for pound, virtually every little panfish that swims is among the scrappiest little fighters in the water, especially on that light tackle I was telling you about. Place the bait or lure anywhere in their vicinity and they'll find it in seconds and strike at it with the force of a daisy-cutter dropping into an Afghan cave. I'm telling you, they mean business when it comes time to eat!

There is a secret to catching them every time, though. When perchjerkin,' *the one thing you never want to do is jerk!* When you feel the strike or you see the float go under the water, just ease back on the rod so that you take the slack out of the line and tension is evenly applied. This is all it really takes to "set the hook" on literally every species of bream and you will rarely if ever miss a fish.

TASTY ON THE TABLE?

You had better believe they are—firm, sweet, white, flaky meat, especially delectable when scaled, gutted and headed, dipped in seasoned cornmeal, and panfried to a crisp, golden, finger-lickin' goodness. Mmm!

Do you fillet them? Capt. Phil Robichaux can (he's got a technique that separates the meat from the bones slicker than a hot knife going through butter), but I like 'em like Paw-Paw showed me—*fried whole!*

So how many are you allowed to catch? Provided you don't pull in any goggle-eyes, yellow bass, white bass, or sac-a-lait (which all have creel limits), you can catch as many perch as you want. Just remember, it's easy to snag 'em and drop 'em in the ol' Igloo, but you've got to clean every single one of them one at a time when you get home.

Why not do this—bring home just enough to whip up a good meal, but leave so many of them behind in the water that you can absolutely guarantee your success the next time you want to do a little "perchjerkin' and panfryin'"!

CHAPTER 4

Jailhouse Snapper

Yeah, right! Go ahead and get all finicky and tell people you'll only eat speckled trout and redfish—you'd never as much as bother fixin' a lowly little sheepshead. But we all know the truth! You're just too lazy to clean 'em. And because of it, you're missing out on some of the best-tasting fish in the water—"Jailhouse Snapper"!

Its scientific name is *Archosargus probatocephalus*. The world-record specimen, according to fish-identification book author Dr. Bob Shipp, was caught in Bayou St. John in New Orleans back in 1982 and tipped the scales at a whopping 21 pounds 4 ounces. It's technically a member of the porgy family, which includes those pesky little pinperch. And it's absolutely delicious to eat, but most people don't or won't for a myriad of excuses!

Found in the coastal waters from the northern Gulf of Mexico all the way up to Nova Scotia, the sheepshead occurs in its thickest concentrations in Florida. But here in Louisiana, what with all our offshore platforms providing reeflike conditions, sheepshead give us not only some excellent fishing possibilities but some equally great *feasting* possibilities as well!

They're one of the only sport fish we have left that can still be caught in "messes": "Hey, Bubba! I done went and caught me a *mess* o' dem sheephaids!"

To accomplish this, though, you have to fish where sheepshead are happiest—in brackish waters around pilings, rock jetties, oil rigs, wellheads, tank batteries, and anywhere there are clams, oysters, barnacles, stone crabs, fiddler crabs, and anything else crunchy enough for them to use their formidable teeth on! Of course, some of the very young juvenile fish prefer to hang out on sandy grassflats, or beachfronts, or smack dab in the middle of a centerline channel, where they snack on "softer foods" like shrimp, squid, and even vegetation.

But even with a set of choppers that one would swear could gnaw straight through bedrock, these fish are persnickety nibble-type eaters with very cautious table manners. They can excise bait from a hook with the subtlety of an urban pickpocket. And because they travel in "schools," their voracious feeding habits can literally drive a beginning fisherman bonkers, causing him to miss bite after bite and sending him back empty hooks over and over and over again!

But sheepshead have always been one of this writer's favorite fish; so perhaps I can offer you a little insight to help you increase your catches.

1. After all these years I've found that the single drop leader is the best rigging you can use to catch sheepshead. Oh, you'll find guys fishin' leadhead jigs, freeline treble hooks, sliding sinker rigs, and whatnot. But a single piece of monofilament folded over (leaving one side twice as long as the other), with a barrel swivel tied in place right at the fold, a snap-swivel and hook on the short end, and a teardrop sinker on the long end, is just plain unbeatable.

2. These fish have razor-sharp gnawing teeth, but they've also got small mouths. So forget about long-shank hooks. Ideally you want to fish with a thick, stout, short-shank blue-steel hook that "won't get in the way of the hook-set" when it's time. In other words, you want as much of the hook as possible inside the fish's mouth. And of course the ultimate is a No. 1 Eagle Claw baitholder or No. 2 Kahle bronze.

3. Respectable-size sheepshead feed very much like Morris the Cat—finicky-like! Even though they pack a good weight and wallop, they do anything but attack the bait. My longtime fishing buddy Pat Armand liked to say that sheepshead

"lipped" the bait. "Musta been a sheepshead bite, Frank! I just felt a couple of fish lips swim up, pucker in a pout, and suck down the market shrimp in one slurp!" he would say. Now that I think about it, Pat probably described the bite of a sheepshead better than any biologist I know.

So if you want to catch them consistently, you'd better not wait for a bite. I suggest you set the hook when *all of a sudden, right in the middle of fishing, your line goes heavy—kinda like you just an instant ago snagged into a piling.* If at that moment you set the hook hard, you'll have yourself a sheepshead to do battle with on the other end of the monofilament. And that's guaranteed!

One other thing—sheepshead are a species that "stratify," which means the entire school will pick a level in the water at which to feed. Usually, they won't swim above or below that level to pursue a bait. So in order to catch them fast and furiously, you'll first have to find out which depth they're holding at, then you'll have to fish that depth on every bait. A little rubber band half-hitched around the monofilament at the reel is a good way of marking the line depth.

But let's get to the real story here. Catchin' 'em ain't the dig! It's cleaning 'em! You always throw 'em back because you think they're hard to clean. Forget that the quality of the fillet is rated "above excellent"! Never mind that the texture is better than snapper. And who cares if the taste of the flesh is incomparable? You're probably going to throw 'em back because you think they're a pain in the behonkers to clean! Right?

Follow this, okay?

Go to the hardware store and buy yourself a linoleum knife—that's the one with the curved arched point on the end of the blade. Then lay out the fish with its head to your left and its tail to your right. From here on it's merely a matter of following a few simple steps:

1. Stick the knife point behind the head at the top of the dorsal. Then cut through to the backbone spine (using the knife point). Next, cut an arc from the lateral line down to the anal fin, bypassing the ribs and the entire belly section.

Repeat the same procedure on the other fillet on the other side.

2. Now take the tip of the knife, go back to the starting point, and begin cutting along the dorsal fin to the tail, going into the flesh about a half-inch. Do this on both sides of the fish, holding the knife blade parallel to the backbone for best technique.

3. Then put the tip of the knife at the exit point at the anal vent and cut down from the anal fin to the tail, again holding the knife blade parallel to the backbone.

4. Finally, put the linoleum knife down and pick up your regular filleting knife. Using the fish's backbone as a guide, take the tip of the filleting knife and slice the fillet off each side of the sheepshead in one fell swoop! Sounds simple, don't it? And if you noticed, if you've done it right you won't have broken open the belly cavity and you will have left the rib bones attached to the backbone! Oh, obviously you remove the flesh from the scales in the same manner as you would fillet a trout. And to produce the ultimate in taste, be certain you trim away every trace of the bloodline!

When you're done cutting, your fillet should look just like a fillet from a prized speckled trout. If it does, bravo—you probably should have been a brain surgeon!

In all honesty, it is going to take you a few days of practice before you get it right. But once you do—*and it really is easy to master*—you won't ever throw back what many gourmands consider to be the most succulent-tasting fish that swims!

On the other hand, let's say you'd just as soon not mess with these pesky little varmints. Just call me and I'll come over to your house to take them off your hands.

CHAPTER 5

Catchin' Croakers

The French call them *tambour*. The Germans call them *adler-fisch*. In Spanish they're known as *corbina*. And the Japanese refer to them as *nibe*. But regardless of your heritage, here in Southeast Louisiana you probably know them best as chut, grunters, rocodina, or—better yet—croakers.

They account for some of the most vivid memories of my childhood. Every Saturday and Sunday, almost year round, Mom and Dad and Grandma and Uncle Mac would drive to Strenge's Place at Irish Bayou, where they'd rent a skiff, load it with Jax and Falstaff ice chests, chill down the Barq's Root Beer and the luncheon meat, wrap the po'-boy bread in a plastic raincoat so that the "splash" wouldn't ruin the loaf, rig handlines with double drops and No. 10 hooks, and portion out the three pounds of dead shrimp they always brought along.

Then first with the old Neptune and later with the 10-horsepower Johnson, they'd head for the second firebreak at the wooden railroad trestle to fill every ice chest on the boat.

Whenever Dad checked the weather and deemed the seas "not too rough for me" (which was the case most of the time), I went along. It got to a point where I just couldn't wait for weekends to come, because every Saturday and Sunday for as long as I can remember the Davis family went "croaker fishing."

Oh, we would catch the occasional speckled trout, redfish, or flounder, but those weren't the fish we were after—we wanted those little, sweetmeat croakers, because back in the late forties and early fifties, croakers were the protein food staple for many New Orleans families. It was the fish you scaled, gutted, and panfried whole to fill you up come suppertime.

And it's amazing just how many veteran "strictly trout" fishermen still remember the little fish in that regard today!

Officially labeled as a member of the Sciaenidae family, which includes sand drum, channel mullet, black drum, speckled trout, white trout, redfish, and spot, the fish is technically identified as "Atlantic croaker." Its scientific name is *Micropogonias undulatus,* and its species ranks among the top three in biomass in existence (the other two being mullets and smaller anchovies).

Scientists believe that adult croakers move into the bays in spring and leave for deeper water in fall. It appears that they spawn in the shallow gulf from October to December. Their larvae then enter the bays, where they spend the first summer in brackish water, usually on muddy bottoms. Within the next year and a half they exist as true bottom feeders, thriving on shrimp, crabs, mollusks, and worms.

But get this!

According to data compiled by the U.S. Fish and Wildlife Service and the Louisiana Department of Wildlife and Fisheries, croakers grow fast but as a species are rather short-lived. The statistics say that most of the fish spawn then die at the end of their second year. In the gulf, they seldom reach over two pounds on the average, compared to their four- and five-pound cousins along the Chesapeake Bay. The so-called "bull croakers" that once dominated the water column out of Empire and Grand Isle appear to be no more. While there are theories, no one really knows for certain what happened to the big fish. When "bulls" are caught these days, they usually come from an area just below the mouth of the Mississippi River.

Regardless of its size, the croaker "croaks" by vibrating strong muscles against its swim bladder, which acts as a resonating chamber much like a drum. Occasionally, old-timers make reference to a fish they call the "golden croaker." Actually, the golden croaker is nothing more than the Atlantic croaker wearing its spawning coloration.

Croakers have three major reasons for their continued popularity, especially along coastal Louisiana.

First, they're a really tasty food fish. You probably heard your grandpa call them the poor man's saltwater perch. The flesh is semifirm and retains its natural sweetness regardless of how it is cooked. Baking, broiling, grilling, bronzing, and pan-frying are common methods of preparation.

If you prefer to panfry your croakers (which is a popular way to fix them here), scale and gut them, cut off the heads, remove the innards, wash away the blood along the back-bones, dredge them in some of my gourmet seasoned fish fry while they're still wet, and drop them into hot 375-degree vegetable oil. When they're done, take a fork and remove the skin (unless you're one of those people who relish the flavor of the skin) to get to the flaky portion called the "loin." This is the flesh above the lateral line, between the backbone and the dorsal fin. But be careful of the belly flaps—which are where all the tiny pin bones are.

Secondly, croakers—especially very small croakers—are probably ranked the number-one live bait for catching monster-size speckled trout. That's because speckled trout and croakers are archenemies. See, in the natural order of things, those pesky croakers presumably attack and eat the speckled trout's eggs. Trout hate it when that happens! So they take out a croaker whenever they can. And if you, as a fisherman, just so happen to have one free-swimming on the bottom with a 3/0 Kahle hook through its lips, well . . . !

Baby croakers are best caught with a cast net or small hand-lines baited with tiny pieces of shrimp. It is imperative that you treat the water in your live well if you intend to keep baby croakers alive for any length of time. That's because they secrete copious amounts of urea, which taints the water and lowers oxygen levels. Baby croakers are very good bait for still fishing, but they don't troll well at all.

Larger croakers that you'll want to dish up at your family fish fry usually take up residence around bridges, over oyster reefs (although you'll tear up a net pretty badly throwing it here!), and in main channels, passes, and cuts. October through December are the hottest months to fish for them since that period constitutes dating season, but they can usually be found somewhere along the coast at almost any time of the year. Once again, small tidbits of market shrimp are your best bait.

Old-timers will tell you that a Carolina or single drop rig are equally effective in putting table croakers in the icebox. The real trick is going with a small enough hook to increase the snare potential (I recommend straight shank hooks instead of Kahle hooks for drop rigging). And don't pile on "chucks" of market shrimp. Small pieces that tip just the barb will catch more croakers than will a wad. Remember, you're not interested in feeding them—you want to catch them!

According to the official Louisiana State Records, the biggest croaker on the charts is an 8-pound whopper caught in August of 1972 by Douglas Bertrand. The number-two fish belongs to Bernard Kabel, weighed 6.29 pounds, and was taken in West Delta in July of 1997. And Joe Turlick, who caught a 5.32-pound record croaker in West Delta in March 1997, holds third-place honors.

Finally we're obviously not the only peoples who love Atlantic croakers. If you check the Internet these days, a company named Saxon has posted an announcement that reads, "Excellent opportunity for Asian and Middle-Eastern countries . . . Atlantic croaker, 100-200 grams through 400-900 grams in the whole round . . . excellent pricing and available for immediate shipment."

Tell me something! Is it just me, or does it seem as if it's just not the same as it was when we used to handline those little critters every Saturday and Sunday way back when we fished from rented skiffs at Strenge's?

CHAPTER 6

The Tackle Box Exam

(DO YOU FIT THE DESCRIPTION?)

Nine wiener-size topwater plugs covered in lavender fake fur and dangling six sets of treble hooks that you bought for a nickel apiece when the Western Auto store closed down, all 10 pounds of lead sinkers the Water Gremlin salesman gave you at the close of last year's Sportsman's Show, and 271 different-colored H&H plastic Cocahoe tails your wife picked up for three dollars at a garage sale. If that's what's in your trays and bins, you seriously need to clean out your tackle box!

Assuming you agree that there might be "the perfect cup of coffee," "the perfect day," "the perfect opportunity," and "the perfect 10," you will certainly also agree that to date no one yet has invented "the perfect tackle box." If you're like me, you must have bought over 25 tackle boxes in your lifetime: small ones, large ones, magnum ones, hard plastic ones with bins, hard plastic ones with trays, hard plastic ones with boxes, canvas ones with boxes, canvas ones that look like duffel bags, duffel bags that look like tackle boxes, ice chests that double as duffel bags and tackle boxes, and so forth and so on! I don't know what it is, but it's as if fishermen could put a handle on a dumpster and still couldn't get all the tackle in it that we'd need on a typical fishing trip.

Unless you are terminally fastidious, your tackle box is either understocked or overstocked. You either have a construction worker's lunchbox-type tackle box containing three rusty hooks, a smushed cork, four bass worms chemically fused into the upper plastic tray, and the crumpled empty sleeve that your Band-Aids came in, or you have three magnum tackle boxes loaded to the rupture point with at least one of every piece of fishing and boating paraphernalia ever to come off the manufacturers' assembly lines. Does that sound about right?

CHAPTER 7

I Caught Another One of Those $%#@*!

Steel gray on top, silvery white on the bottom, feathery wisps trailing off its fins, ever ready to slime up at least two feet of the leader above the hook that snares it, considered a major courtbouillon ingredient once its bloodline is trimmed away, and determined to relentlessly fight its captors from first bite all the way to the boat, the gafftop catfish still invokes one and only one comment amongst every fishermen it comes up against . . . "I Caught Another One of Those $%#@*!"

It was that unmistakable thud—almost like the sound you hear when you thump a ripe watermelon. That's what I sensed in the monofilament when the fish bit!

"Awww, man! I can tell you right now," I moaned, "this is not a big trout. I done caught another one of those $%#@*!"

The biological translation of $%#@* is sailcat, gafftop, top-gaff, topgaffsail, or gafftopsail, which to the average sportfisherman is all the same thing—a catfish! Oh, maybe not a pesky hardhead, but a catfish nonetheless. And to the scientifically nondiscriminating, catfish are catfish are catfish . . . period. But that's not exactly true!

All across Louisiana's coastline, the waters from deep inside Barataria all the way out to the platforms in Breton Sound are teeming with the cats. But unlike their cousins the hardheads, gafftops for the most part are a sought-after species. Clean and dress them properly and you have excellent tablefare, fried, grilled, barbecued, baked, broiled, bronzed, or blackened.

Oh—and just ask anyone who knows his courtbouillon and he'll tell you none is tastier than one made with gafftops.

So where do you find them? How do you catch them? And what do you have to know about them? Let's start at the beginning.

THE BIOLOGY

The gafftop, *Bagre marinus,* is one of only two marine (saltwater) catfishes that inhabit the Gulf of Mexico (and you already know what that other $%#@*! is). It is a true predator and an extremely aggressive feeder, which makes it, for all practical purposes, a game fish. Long billowy filaments flow from its dorsal and pectoral fins (hence the name "sailcat"), and its skin is covered in a slimy mucous that protects it from parasites and infections. The mucous is one of its distinguishing marks—hook a gafftop and, in its gyrations to shake the hook, it will "slime" about two feet of your line and leader.

The fish is a true *mouthbreeder.* Males carry their young inside their mouths, providing for them a place to grow and hide from danger. The process starts each year in May, when the eggs, which are about the size of mothballs, are "dropped" by the female and are immediately fertilized and picked up by the male.

After about 60 days, the young, nearly an inch long, hatch out, and for the next couple of months as many as 25 to 50 of them will take refuge inside ol' Dad's jaws. Obviously, for fear of losing his family, Dad doesn't eat at all during this time!

WHERE ARE THEY FOUND?

Gafftops are very sensitive to cold, so during the winter months, especially November, December, and January, they migrate offshore to the deeper, warmer waters of the gulf. But they begin heading back into the Louisiana estuaries in March, April, and May.

Throughout the summer they hang out in main tidal channels, in deep holes on the marsh, and under oil platforms.

They'll readily take natural bait (cut fish, squid, market shrimp, live Cocahoes, small crabs, and shiners); but because of their predatory nature they'll also strike at artificial lures (plastic grubs, split-tail beetles, Cocahoe tails, Sassy Shads, you name it!).

HOW ARE THEY CAUGHT?

Because they are primarily bottom feeders, the best method of catching them is by "bottom-fishing." Using either baitcasting or spinning tackle, most fishermen use about 20-pound-test monofilament tied to a 30-pound-test shock leader. Terminal rigging can be of several configurations:

1. Either a single leader, attached to the main monofilament with a swivel, fitted with a 2/0 Kahle hook, and weighted down with a quarter-ounce sliding sinker above the swivel;

2. A single drop rig, with a three-eighths-ounce teardrop sinker on the main lead and a 3/0 long-shank hook off the shorter lead, each of them attached to a barrel swivel that is connected to the main monofilament; or

3. Just a quarter-ounce or half-ounce jig head tied directly to the monofilament.

If you fish with live bait, just hook up and toss it out, giving the bait time to get to the bottom. You might occasionally want to pop the bait once or twice just to attract the fish's attention.

If you'd rather fish with market (dead) bait, hook up, toss out, and let the rigging settle to the bottom. Then pop or twitch the line every few seconds or so to cause the bait to be highly visible to the fish.

Of course, if you decide to use plastic artificials, fish them with the same techniques you'd use for trout and redfish. Simply bounce the jig off the bottom by gently twitching the rod tip as you reel in the line a little at a time with an irregular retrieve.

The real trick is to keep the line tight all the time, ever ready for the bite. Gafftops hit at the bait with a powerful thud, so it's easier to hook them just as they strike (they tend not to completely swallow the hook this way) as opposed to waiting for them to take the bait and swim away.

Depending upon its size, which usually averages about a foot or so and several pounds, the fish can be a formidable foe. It can be brutal in its attempt to throw the hook and is known for its slow, steady, but powerful runs, usually in one direction. More often than not, it also likes to dive and run directly under the boat when it realizes it is losing the battle.

One note here: gafftops are definitely capable of producing a painful sting with their dorsal and pectoral fins, but because they are so much bigger than their squirmy, hardhead cousins, and because there is also a significant degree of protection from the "sails" trailing off their spines, that is not so likely to happen. In short, they're easier to handle than hardheads, but I still suggest you handle them with care!

HOTSPOTS IN LOUISIANA

Gafftops are likely to be wherever the water is saltiest and wherever you find a nice deep hole or some definitive structure. If you really want to catch them, forget about the so-called hotspots and concentrate on strategy. The best way to catch these fish consistently is to find them clustered in a school. Unfortunately, it may take a little patience to pull this off, because sometimes you have to sift through what seems like hundreds of worthless hardheads to catch a few decent gaffs. But if you happen to luck out and anchor over a school of just gafftops, get ready for some heated action. On the right tackle—*light tackle!*—these guys definitely put up a decent fight. You also need to be aware that, when last I looked, the gafftop is one of the fish species on the Coastal Conservation Association Fishing Rodeo Roster that's worth the prize of a boat, motor, and trailer.

HOW GOOD ARE THEY TO EAT?

As I noted earlier in this chapter, most fishermen agree that gafftops make for pretty good dining! But regardless of which method of preparation you intend to use, it is essential that one thing be done without fail. *The heavy bloodline must be meticulously trimmed off the fillets!* If it isn't, the finished dishes you prepare from the meat will taste pungent and fishy. With the bloodline removed, however, the fillets take on a sweet, mild flavor (which is why the Cajuns prefer gafftops for their famed courtbouillon).

One more thing—it's not necessary to skin gafftops as you skin freshwater catfish. They usta do that in the old days. Today's fishermen don't do that anymore. We found that gafftops come out perfectly fine just being filleted, much the same as you would fillet speckled trout.

THE RECORD FISH!

Finally, according to current statistics, the International Game Fish Association World Record for gafftop catfish stands at 8 pounds 14 ounces. That particular fish was taken out of Indian River in Florida on September 21, 1996, by Larry C. Jones. Obviously, it must have been caught on superlight line or something, because even right here in Louisiana the record held by Elie Pellegrin is for an 11-pound 1-ounce gaff caught in October 1996 in Redfish Bayou. And that's a big gafftop!

But I don't know. After checking the Louisiana Fish Records List I noticed that there's only one place—first place—occupied in the state records. So I've decided that the very next nine gafftops I catch will all be photographed, weighed, verified for species by a certified Wildlife and Fisheries biologist, and submitted to the Louisiana Outdoor Writers Association as record fish!

So okay, maybe they won't hold up for any length of time, but that's all right with me. All it means is I got a chance to get back out on the water and catch another one of those $%#@*!

CHAPTER 8

You Gotta Give 'Em What They Want

I wish I had a nickel every time I heard a fisherman say, "You can't use a popping cork in the winter!" Or "You'll never get a redfish to bite on a Cocahoe if you put it on a jig head!" Or "I never heard of using a split-shot to catch speckled trout over an oyster reef!" These are the kinds of statements "bad-luck fishermen" make, you know, the ones who come back to the launch time and again after fishing all day only to tell everyone that they didn't catch anything because they just had "a streak of bad luck!" Well, that's really not an accurate assessment. More than likely, these guys just never learned that to catch fish consistently . . . "You Gotta Give 'Em What They Want"!

The pros, the veterans, the guides, the guys whose names show up year after year as winners on the rodeo tote boards will tell you with zero reservation (if you could pry it out of them) that you're going to catch fish only if you're willing to be versatile enough to play the game by the fish's rules! Let me explain.

Say you leave the house on any given Saturday morning, hell-bent and determined that this day you're only going to fish cast-and-retrieve with a single quarter-ounce jig head fitted with a Mister Twister silver and black swimming grub tied directly to the monofilament. Well, be sure you pass by a Popeye's Chicken on your way home. You'll need to pick up the "special" if you're planning to eat supper, because odds are you won't be dining on trout or redfish!

Let me take you back even further than that, to the point where this entire mental attitude starts.

When all of us were young whippersnappers, we absorbed fishing information like sponges from the "top-gun" anglers we met at the marinas and boat launches. These were the guys who knew! These guys always caught fish! And if by chance they happened, by a slip of the lip, to allow us to overhear one of their fishin' secrets, we took it as gospel! And those were the techniques and tactics we patterned our personal fishing styles after all these years.

Of course, all that holy writ might have been appropriate way back in the early fifties, but as we headed into the new millennium, the ecology and the environment changed such that much of it just didn't (and doesn't) apply anymore.

For example, the Speck-A-Go-Go, the Pluggin' Shorty, and the Shad Rig are now virtually obsolete. The late-forties statement that redfish only bite in wintertime is passe. Even the prolific croakers of the bygone Irish Bayou heyday rarely show up anymore. So all in all it's time we adopted new attitudes. And Attitude Number One, when it comes to putting fish in the boat, is . . . *you gotta give 'em what they want.*

Regardless of the season, the time of the year, the direction of the wind, the temperature of the air, the color of the water, the lay of the shoreline, the strength of the tide, and the fullness of the moon, only the fish itself will determine how, when, where, and why it will take a bait. So for you to ensure that you'll catch fish, you had better present the bait the way the fish wants it, not the way your stubborn nature dictates. Here are the specifics:

• First try your favorite artificial on a common, unpainted, quarter-ounce leadhead jig.

• Try casting it against the shoreline and slowly bringing it back to the boat on a straight retrieve.

• Then try making the cast toward the shoreline and bringing it back to the boat on a twitchy, jerky retrieve. Then make a cast and try "ripping" it through the water as fast as you can wind. If that doesn't work, on the next cast try popping it easy then pausing. Then try popping it hard and pausing.

• If you get no strikes doing this, do a 180 in the boat and begin casting away from the shoreline out into open water (sometimes fish hang and feed out from the bank in deeper water). Again, use the straight retrieve (both fast and slow), the twitch, and the pop. Test each one to see which, if any, will produce a bite.

• Next, repeat the whole process using a different kind and color artificial lure. You might want to tie on a lighter jig head (go from a quarter-ounce to a one-eighth ounce) to see if that changes the action of the lure, thus enticing a strike.

• Suppose, though, that none of that works. Then next you'll want to replicate the entire process, but this time using a live Cocahoe minnow instead of a plastic lure. It's perfectly okay to put a minnow on the leadhead jig and fish that method. Once the live bait is in place, treat it exactly the way you would handle an artificial—cast-and-retrieved, popped, jerked, and twitched. But try this also: just make the cast and *let the minnow sit!* Quite often you'll prompt more response by simply letting the minnow do what it does naturally. Don't pop it, don't jerk it, don't move it at all. Let it sit!

• But let's say the jig-head technique isn't working. Then you should switch to a sliding sinker (Carolina rig). For trout, redfish, or flounder, a live Cocahoe or live shrimp is your bait of choice. Just make the cast, let the minnow sit, and take up the slack as it develops. For redfish, drum, sheepshead, flounder, and other bottom fish, you can also use market shrimp in place of live bait. It sometimes outperforms the live stuff.

• The ultimate live bait presentation, however, is the free-line technique. Simply executed, you tie a 2/0 or 3/0 Kahle hook directly to the terminal end of the monofilament. Then you bait the hook with a live Cocahoe. Then about six inches above the baited hook you pinch on a one-eighth- or one-quarter-ounce split-shot. Then you make your cast first against the shoreline, then out toward open water, and allow the hooked minnow to swim freely in the current. This is one of the most free-spirited techniques in fishing and ranks right at the top of the tactics for catching big trout (when the fish picks up the minnow all you'll feel is the line straighten out). It is most probably a personal choice but I tend to enjoy free-lining best on a spinning outfit as opposed to a baitcasting one. I find I get fewer backlashes with the lighter rigging.

• And finally, there's the old reliable cork. When you get no bites and no fish by fishing bottom, don't be reluctant to tie on a cork—*regardless of what time of year it is!* You can use a popping cork, a chugging cork, or a rattling cork. Just tie it on so that the bait—either live or artificial—dangles at some predetermined depth between the surface and the bottom (usually 18 inches below the surface is a good place to start).

• Veteran fishermen will tell you that, regardless of where you fish, there are very few combinations more productive than a cork and a chartreuse split-tail beetle. But you can match up the cork with H&H Cocahoe tails, the smoke-flake Deadly Dudley Junior, the various grub-style baits, and even the infamous shrimp worms. As with the bottom rigging, make your cast and, first, try popping and chugging it hard; then, secondly, make your cast and just let the baited cork sit in the current. Occasionally, especially during low-water periods, chugging and popping the cork achieves just the reverse of what it is supposed to: instead of attracting fish to the sound, it spooks them and chases them away. So try the cork both ways.

• I know that all this sounds like an insurmountable task, leaving absolutely no fun in fishin'! But that's just the way it sounds. I've belabored it to make the point. But executing the techniques properly does not require much effort at all.

• In the first place, you'll need to try all these different techniques at only four times during the year (all the other times are usually drop-dead simple). You'll have to diversify this much only at what's called "the transitional seasons"— winter to spring, spring to summer, summer to fall, and fall to winter. It is at these times when the fish are confused about what they are supposed to be doing "naturally." Is it winter? Is it spring? It's April, but yesterday a cold front dropped the water temperature as if it was mid-December! The fisherman's key word at these times is compensation, or as my ol' fishin' buddy usta say, "Ya go with the flow!"

Of course, the easiest way to accommodate the diversification is to bring along several rods and reels. The last thing you want to do is spend all day changing baits, tying and retying rigging, and putting on and taking off different configurations. One rod and reel rigged for cork fishing, one Carolina-rigged for bottom-fishing, one rigged for jig-head cast-and-retrieve, and one more rigged for freelining and you're ready to negotiate just about any circumstance (and catch some serious fish to boot).

In other words, you'll be ready to . . . "give 'em what they want!"

CHAPTER 9

Oh, My God, I'm Getting Seasick

The late great outdoor writer Paul Kalman once told me that it's one of those illness where you know you'll have to die in order to feel better. I'm here to tell you, though, that you never have to be seasick ever again!

With every crest and every valley in every wave, relentlessly for hours on end, the boat rises and falls, rhythmically rocking from side to side. First you experience only a slight sense of dizziness, but you take in a few deep oxygen-rich breaths and the feeling goes away.

But within moments, it comes back again, only this time it is more intense. Along with the dizziness you now feel clammy and somewhat chilled. Your face begins to tingle and you get the sensation of a headache starting. Minutes later you find yourself yawning uncontrollably, the diesel stinks like you've never smelled before, and then the nausea sets in. Instantly you realize that there's no way you're going to keep your bacon and eggs down! And as the sweat pours down your collar you whisper to yourself, *"Oh, my God, I'm getting seasick!"*

According to all the medical journals, the condition is technically termed *mal de mer,* an age-old physical disturbance affecting the inner ear and induced by significant motion disorientation that results in moderate to severe nausea and vomiting.

But when you get right down to the nitty-gritty, and when you're bouncing around in five-foot seas on your brother-in-law's boat just off the rocks at Shell Beach or in the breakers at

East Timbalier Island, you call it "seasickness." And it's one of the most God-awful experiences you'll ever have.

So in this chapter of *The Bible*, I'll give you the latest facts about seasickness and some tips to help you avoid this miserable affliction.

1. Most often, seasickness occurs when an individual views rapidly moving surroundings or when positional orientation is impaired (as when watching a leaping horizon).

2. Seasickness, most authorities agree, seems to be triggered by the mechanisms of the "inner ear." This intricate piece of human anatomy gives you your sense of balance and operates very much like a brick-mason's level. Paul Kalman once told me that he found out in his investigations that fluids circulating in the inner ear pass over extremely sensitive nerve endings connected to the brain. When the fluids move in different directions, the nerves over which they pass send signals to your motor reflexes, causing extremities and other portions of the body to take counteractive measures to keep you in balance. Any disturbance in this complicated system throws you out of balance and, consequently, projects you into a condition of nausea.

3. Recent research has shown that several things bring about equilibrium upset: infection, anxiety, violent motion, fatigue, and alcoholic beverages. Eliminating the causes most often eliminates the onset of seasickness.

4. Food and beverage intake prior to going on a boat often is critical if you want to avoid motion nausea. While *what* you eat and drink isn't nearly so important as *how much* you eat and drink, it is a good idea to avoid a so-called *hearty breakfast*. Oh, do eat breakfast, but confine it to such foods as dry toast, crackers, cereal, oatmeal, bananas, and other solids that will put a foundation in your stomach. Stay away from greasy fried eggs, bacon or sausage that isn't cooked supercrisp, toast drenched in butter, orange juice, and several cups of coffee.

5. Some folks make it a rule not to eat anything before going on a boat. The authorities say this is utterly ridiculous;

seasickness is much worse on an empty stomach (it's hard to toss your cookies if you got no cookies to toss!).

6. Probably more critical than a greasy breakfast, though, is the partying you do the night before a fishing trip. Lack of sleep and too much hooch can bring about *mal de mer* faster than anything you've ever seen.

7. No doubt about it, the best treatment for seasickness is "terra firma," getting the seasick person back on solid ground. It's remarkable how quickly the symptoms disappear when you are standing on something that doesn't move! But if solid ground is some distance away (and besides, charter-boat captains—*and your brother-in-law*—never head back to port just because one passenger aboard gets woozy), there are things you can do to alleviate the misery.

8. Get busy doing something that takes your mind off the rolling boat, the choppy seas, and the jumping horizon. Don't look at the horizon or anything else that accentuates movement of the boat. Select a spot onboard (the center preferably) where motion is minimal. It always helps to find a breezy spot, too, in the fresh air (stay out of the cabin if you can help it!), and get something cool and nonalcoholic to drink. You might also try eating about a half-dozen or so dry crackers.

But if none of the preceding remedies helps, then go into the cabin, lie on your back in the lowest spot you can find, and close your eyes. You'll be amazed how the severity of nausea decreases. While you're lying there, talk yourself out of being sick, telling yourself that you are just nervous, and nauseous because of it, and that when you get up in a few minutes you'll be just fine.

It is easy to recognize the symptoms of beginning *mal de mer:* excessive yawning, depression, profuse cold sweats, waning of attention, too-rapid breathing, a greenish pallor, hiccuping, a strong urge to carry out all your bodily functions at the same time, and—at the end—an almost irresistible desire to jump overboard and drown yourself! Develop these signs and you're in deep doo-doo!

There is one thing you got to know, though. Everybody, but everybody, is capable of becoming seasick at any time. You've met these people who boast, "I never get seasick!" Well, your response should always be, "Well, maybe not yet!" This is the malady for which the expression "never say never" was coined.

And now it's confession time. You've seen me on television every week as well as in person at marinas and boat launches, climbing aboard practically every kind of boat ever built. Well, the truth of the matter is . . . *I get seasick in the shower!*

So I practice those tips I've just passed along to you, but I also take it a step farther. Every trip I make on the water, whether it be for fun fishing with my family on the weekends or shooting my weekly television shows, I take what over the years I've found to be the absolute best seasick medication ever to hit the market.

My old friend By Hek told me about it over 30 years ago and I haven't been seasick since. It's called *TripTone,* it's available over the counter at most drugstores, and it's a buffered, time-release medication similar to Dramamine. But since it is time released, unlike Dramamine it doesn't make you sleepy! It's the only product I've found on the market that really and truly works for fishermen.

So you see, there isn't any need to give up fishing just because you get queasy. Just closely follow the guidelines and always take your TripTone. The only thing you'll really give up is feeding the fish from the top!

CHAPTER 10

Outfitted for Fishin'

The man had been following in my tracks for at least a half-hour. I couldn't help but feel that he wanted to say something, but whenever I made eye contact with him he pulled back, pretending to direct his attentions elsewhere.

Finally, as I moved into that little chutelike aisle that the point-of-purchase racks form at the check-out counter, he rushed up behind me and blurted out, "Frank Davis, can I talk with you for a minute?"

As the cashier swooshed my grocery items over the laser scanner, the man apologized for stalking me in the produce section, staring at me back at the dairy case, and tailing me from the soft-drink racks over to the mayonnaise display. He explained that at first he wasn't quite sure it was me, so he refrained from saying anything out of embarrassment. Then he explained that after he was convinced it *was* me, he still shied away from a conversation because he didn't want to be bothersome. But then he said that when he saw me about to check out and leave the store, he just had to speak up in a last-ditch effort.

"I got something I want you to consider. We all watch you catch fish on TV every week. So why don't you write an article for us that tells us exactly what you use to catch fish? I don't mean in generalities—I mean, tell us the kind of reel you use, the kind of rod, the names of the baits, the hook sizes, the boat brands. I mean specifics! I mean, damn, you catch fish

71

with the stuff *you* use. So don't give *me* a bunch of stuff to choose from. Tell me what you use, and that's what I want!"

I got to thinking later, the man had a point. As objective outdoor writers, we're all trained from the get-go to be unbiased and nonendorsing. But when you consider the vast quantities and huge selections of outdoor gear the sportsman has to choose from, we provide very little help and do absolutely no service whatsoever to our readers when we write in objective generalities, telling our readers they can use "either/or."

So in this chapter, I'm going to be biased! I'm going to be specific! I'm going to tell you exactly what's in my fishing arsenal! I'm going to name what I take along with me on every fishing trip and what I use to catch fish. It may not be what Bill Dance or Mark Sosin or Bob Marshall or Phil Robichaux uses. And if you disagree with my methods and my choices . . . fine. I will at least have done what a really nice gentleman I met at the supermarket once asked me to do.

I fish with . . .

• *Four rods and reels on every trip*—one rigged with a single quarter-ounce jig head fitted with a plastic beetle or Cocahoe tail; one fitted with a slip sinker and a Carolina rig attached to a Kahle hook for fishing live bait on the bottom; one rigged only with a snelled Kahle hook tied directly to the monofilament for freelining live bait in the current; and one rigged with a 24-inch shock leader tied under a rattling cork for fishing on the surface. The four individual rods and reels save you valuable time by keeping you from continually having to tie and retie terminal tackle.

• *Reels*—I use both baitcasting and open-face spinning reels. My favorites are the Shimano Calcutta (150 and 250) as well as the Ambassadeur 5000 and 5500. For bass fishing, I throw either the Team Diawa baitcast or the Shimano Stradic 2000.

• *Rods*—I fish only with All-Star, Cast-Away, Tsunami, and Shimano. I also don't use a rod that's under 6 ½ feet (I prefer 7 footers), and every one of them is either medium or heavy action with a fast taper tip (which gives me good hook-setting backbone).

• *Line*—I rarely use anything but Berkley Trilene Big Game or PowerPro braided nylon. In mono, I rig mostly in 10-, 12-, 15-, and 17-pound test. In PowerPro I prefer 30-pound test (which actually has a casting diameter equivalent to 8-pound test). A few of my reels are loaded with 20-pound-test mono for redfish on the marsh. And several of my freshwater reels are fitted with the new Excalibur line because of its abrasion resistance.

• *Plastic bait*—For saltwater, I use both the regular and queen-size H&H Cocahoe tails as well as the split-tail beetles and salty grubs, and the plastic shad made by Mister Twister. I also like the Deadly Dudley as well as the brand-new Hybrids Flurrys made by Edge Products in California. I heartily recommend, however, that you forget about filling your tackle box with 796 different colors—all you really need are a few basics. In the beetle I prefer smoke, white with the red hotspot, motor oil, chartreuse, avocado, glo-glitter, purple with the white tail, and black with the chartreuse tail. In the Cocahoe, you'll need smoke glitter, white, motor oil, tuxedo, chartreuse, avocado, glow, solid purple, black with the chartreuse tail, and chartreuse with the black back. In the Hybrids, key-lime and lit-up are probably my favorites, and if I'm after big trout in the lake I regularly tie on a Fearless Frank or Blue-Moon Deadly Dudley. For freshwater, I fish bass with only the Fishin' Delite PowerPede worms—purple, plum, black, blue, junebug, and bubblegum. I hardly ever use spinnerbaits, and I only use buzzbaits—white and chartreuse only—on those really slick mornings in the early spring and summer.

• *Hard plastics*—I hardly ever use them either. But I do carry along the Zara Spook topwater as well as the H&H Skipjack and Rattlin Stick in both the silver and blue and the green and white color pattern for when the big trout and redfish are up shallow.

• *Jig heads*—I use only the round, unpainted H&H brand in

quarter-ounce, three-eighths-ounce, and half-ounce weights. After all these years I've found that there's really no proof that painted heads are needed.

• *Sinkers*—I also use H&H quarter-ounce and half-ounce egg sinkers for making Carolina rigs, Water Gator rubbercore sinkers for bottom-fishing, and Water Gator needle-nose weights for worm fishing. You should always carry a good assortment of these.

• *Rigging*—I never use a swivel except on a Carolina rig fitted to a slip sinker or on a double or triple drop when I'm offshore fishing snapper or bottom fish at the rigs. Oh—and never use a snap swivel on a leadhead jig—always, always tie the lure directly to the monofilament. And where leaders are concerned, I usually make my own from Trilene Big Game 30-pound-test monofilament or American Fishing Tie-able Wire fitted with compression sleeves.

Aside from all the above, I also carry a magnum tackle box fully stocked with gear for all kinds of fishing, and a small tackle bag (which I fondly refer to as my RBFOS—red bag full of stuff). In the tackle box I have the individual plastic trays full of bait and tackle; in the upper "bin section" I stash the pliers, screwdriver, scale, fillet knife, extra spool of line, and miscellaneous hardware. In the RBFOS, I carry a bug suit, rain suit, windbreaker, Polaroid sunglasses, GPS unit, small camera, pointy-nose pliers, wire cutters, and sunscreen. Anything else you pack is purely personal choice.

Let me make one more efficiency recommendation. I suggest you also make a "Fishin' Trip List" and post it in some conspicuous place in your house. On it you should write down everything you always want to have with you on every single trip—the tackle box, RBFOS, cap, sunglasses, pocket knife, needle-nose pliers, fishing towel, extra pair of socks, camera, extra film, chewing gum . . . get the picture?

Oh, by the way, I saw the man from the supermarket again just the other day. I told him I was writing the article and I promised him that the information I was providing had worked flawlessly for me for over 35 years. He told me he couldn't wait to read it. But this time he also wanted to know if he could call me personally from time to time if he ever had any questions about what I wrote.

Hey, I'm a nice guy! Why don't y'all write it down too? The number is 504-529-6431. My assistant's name is Gail and she always knows where to find me!

CHAPTER 11

Hook-'n'-Line Crabbin'

A rod and reel, a handline, a Carolina rig, maybe just a jig head tied directly to the monofilament, even just a string knotted around a chicken neck! Any of these devices, a long-handled dip net, and a little bit of patience are all you need to go ..."Hook-'n'-Line Crabbin'"!

I rediscovered it purely by accident (or maybe it was just desperation). The winds had been howling for days, there were white caps even back in the duck ponds, none of the adjacent open water bays was fishable, and most of the inside protected canals and bayous were "chocolate-milk dirty."

The only recourse any of us had who were out fishing that particular Thursday was to get deep into the marsh where tides and wind did little to affect water clarity and quality. And that's exactly how Terry Jones, Johnny Glover, and I ended up back at the weir off Lake Boudreaux . . . *catching crabs!*

Actually, we had gone to the weir specifically to cast plastic artificials over to the landlocked side of the old water-control structure to see if we could stir up a couple of flounders (Johnny had been there countless times before and always fished that spot whenever the weather refused to cooperate). After a half-dozen or so casts, and when he was convinced the artificial bait wasn't going to work, Johnny opted to try a live Cocahoe minnow on the bottom. Seconds later he caught the first big male blue crab—it was hanging onto the Cocahoe for dear life, feeding as Johnny slowly eased it toward the boat.

"Got him!" he shouted out, scooping the crab up in the landing net. "Now if I can pull in about a dozen like this, we'll be able to stuff those flounders we're fixin' to catch!"

Of course, flounders were not to be in our forecast. Instead, one lone crab became two crabs, then four crabs. Then one lone crab fisherman became two crab fishermen, then three crab fishermen. It didn't take long before Terry and I both discarded the plastic Cocahoes and hooked on real ones. In no time at all, we had joined Johnny's program.

"Oooh, Frank, look at the size of this guy!" Johnny shouted, winching another big male toward the gunwale and into the outstretched net. "I'm about ready to forget the fish for today and get serious about catching these crabs. These guys are monsters!"

About five minutes later, we had all permanently abandoned the idea of catching any flounders and had seized the opportunity—it was destined to be a "crabbin'" day and we resigned ourselves to go at it with unwavering gusto.

"This kinda thing really happens all the time," Glover explained as we began the collection. "Fishermen come out, the water is too rough for them to get offshore or along the beaches, the surf might be dirty, fish can't find the bait in the stained water, and they end up back here at the dams. Now doubtless they come to fish flounder or school trout or puppy drum, but many many times they accidentally start hauling in crabs and they end up making the crabs the primary quarry. I mean, let's face it—it's hard to quit pulling in one fat crab after another when you know that the alternative is to try and find a spot where you might catch one or two trout!"

Hook-and-line crabbing has always been popular along bayou settlements, and the Chauvin/Cocodrie area is no exception. Trout and red fishermen sometimes tie off along a grassy shoreline to crab with cut bait as an alternative to a poor day's fishing. But most often hook-and-line crabbing is a family activity. Dad first locates a spot where the crabs are thick (kinda like the weir we fished at on our last trip out).

Then he runs back to the house to get the family (most often Mom and the kids) and takes them back to the "secret spot" for some true Cajun quality time and the makings of a neighborhood crabboil. (For the record, at a good spot you can actually pick up enough crabs to feed the whole block—we ended up with 128 and it only took nine Cocahoe minnows to catch 'em!)

Anyway, to make a long story short, by the end of the morning, without us ever realizing it, Johnny, Terry, and I had automatically initiated a buddy-system. We'd ease in our own catch, but for efficiency's sake we'd take turns netting each other's crabs.

"Johnny, Johnny! Get this one! It's the biggest one of the day!" I yelled at the top of my lungs. Like poetry in motion, Glover thrust the net under the crab and snatched him to the boat. "I can't believe we're catching this many with just a hook and a piece of dead minnow! I mean, don't nobody down here use crab nets, or crab cages, or crab traps?"

"Oh, sure," Glover replied, transferring another crab from the dip net to the ice chest in one move, "all the commercial crabbers do. But this isn't commercial crabbing. This is fun crabbing! This is how families do it as recreation. This is interactive—kids really get into this because it's them on one end of the line and the crab on the other. And if they reel too fast or they jerk too hard, the crab is gone!"

Later, back at Coco Marina, we resumed this conversation as we stood around the pot watching the freshly boiled crabs soak up the seasonings. "So is there a right way and a wrong way to do this as family recreation, Johnny?" I asked.

"All you want to do, Frank, is keep it simple!" he explained. "No matter where you live—here or in Lafitte or at Myrtle Grove or on Lake Pontchartrain—you first want to find a likely spot where crabs collect. That could be up against a grassy flat, under an old deserted duck blind, up against a water-control dam, along a drop-off that borders a pier, a dock, or a seawall, or wherever.

"Then you tie up or anchor both ends of the boat so that everyone on board can crab off the sides. You want to be able to just ease the bait over—you don't want to do any casting! Just over the side and all the way to the bottom is the ticket.

"Then as far as tackle is concerned, you can use a rod and reel with a weight above a swivel, a 14-inch shock leader, and a 2-0 hook baited with a dead Cocahoe or chunk of cut mullet. You can also get the job done with a handline, a drop sinker, and a baited hook. And there are some folks who use nothing but a piece of string tied directly to a chicken neck. All you want to do is get the bait into the water, drop it all the way to the bottom, and feel for the 'tug.' When it comes, ever so slowly bring the bait (and the crab that's going to be hanging onto it!) back to the boat and within reach of the net."

Now I do have to admit that initially, on that particular Thursday, I had envisioned a phenomenal macho day on the water, tying into monster trout upwards of eight pounds and bragging about how I intricately wrestled them back to the boat, moments before they each were about to throw the hook.

Of course, once I cracked open the top shell on the first of many spicy boiled crabs that dripped into the newsprint covering the picnic table on Johnny's wharf, popped the top on the first frosty can of imported brewsky, and tasted the richness of that first bite of lump meat right off the flipper, well . . . I realized that one can always catch trout and reds and flounders, but you're truly not a well-rounded, versatile, and accomplished sportsman until you've done something like, oh, say, *"hook-'n'-line crabbin'."*

CHAPTER 12

How to Find Hawg Trout in Lower Barataria

First, you launch at Lafitte, but . . .

Don't stop to make that first cast until you get well into the Lower Barataria System—I'm talking about Queen Bess, Bassa Bassa, Manilla Village, Coupa Bell, Four Bayou Pass, and all the broken islands dotting Barataria Bay. Because that's where seven times out of ten you'll find big schools of "hawg trout."

If you're an artificial-bait aficionado, a quarter-ounce jig head fitted with a white split-tail beetle with a hotspot could be the only lure you need. Fish it directly (and slowly) on the bottom and it should produce strikes one after the other. Here are a few other things that are mandatory.

In addition to using the white split-tail beetle and getting out early, you want to be sure you focus on clean water, water where you have a current working. Clean water and a current line are the two most important prerequisites you can establish in this part of Southeast Louisiana. Also important is how the lures are presented and worked.

I suggest you approach the Barataria islands and subsequent fishing spots very quietly—don't run the big outboard (use your trolling motor or a paddle), keep your voice muffled and subdued, don't go to droppin' noisy objects on the floor of the boat, don't run up on fishermen already in place and fishing. Oh, yeah—and be sure to make an extra effort to fish flat on the bottom.

Fish even a few inches off the bottom and there's a very

good possibility you won't ever feel a bite, let alone catch a fish! It's a critical evaluation, to be sure. What I found out over the years is that you will need to approach the points, cuts, reefs, platforms, and other places of "structure" carefully and quietly, staying about 30 to 40 yards off the shoreline. Then you need to make your casts in virtually every direction from the drifting boat (anchor only when you come upon a feeding school!). Fish straight out front from the bow. Fish all along the port side. Fish straight out back behind the stern. Fish all along the starboard side. In other words, don't miss casting to any one spot! The trout could be just a few feet farther from where your last cast landed.

And there's one more thing you got to do if you plan to engage in some steady action—fish dead slow. No whipping the lure through the water. No rough snapping and jerking the rod tip. Fish these trout the same as you'd fish bass. Allow the lure to sink to the bottom after the cast. Then begin what's best described as a "twitching motion" at the end of the rod. If you can make it appear as though the lure is attempting to sneak away from the trout, the trout will strike it every time! At that point it's then only a matter of setting the hook.

Oh, I have one other strategic point to offer before I end this chapter, regarding *big fish versus little fish*. You need to know that wherever and whenever you fish, they are not all going to be 18, 20, and 24 inches (even though a good number of them in the Lower Barataria really and truly will be!). So when you come up onto a school, determine very quickly which size the majority of the fish in that school will be. You do this by averaging—if the first three or four fish you land are all barely 12 inches, stop casting at that spot and move. Chances are all the fish in that particular school will be "smallies." Immediately scout out another school. If the first three fish you catch there are all over 4 pounds, chances are all the fish in that particular school will be 4 pounds or better! That's how you locate keeper trout and fill your limit with "braggers" only. Find those kind and you can drop anchor and work it a while!

CHAPTER 13

Finding Redfish in the Ponds at Golden Meadow

You seldom have to go very far from Chick's Launch at Golden Meadow to find big schools of cruising redfish. Every veteran fisherman will tell you that they usually hang out in all of the adjacent brackish-marsh duck ponds, where they spend the better part of the day chasing shrimp and minnows.

Here are some points to keep in mind when you go after them:

1. Fish up against the grass lines about 14 inches under a cork and use live Cocahoes for bait.

2. Toss as close to the bank as you can get—most of the fish will hold tight to the shoreline.

3. When the minnow is struck and killed, replace it with a fresh lively one—redfish are adamant about wanting live and lively bait.

4. Concentrate on pockets, points, reefs, broken islands, and grass tufts. Science tells us that those are the dominant congregating places (especially in duck ponds).

5. Make long casts. This will require you to stay some distance off the shoreline so as not to spook the fish in the shallow water.

6. Use your trolling motor to position yourself into casting range and to allow yourself to scout the bank. If you don't have a trolling motor, position yourself parallel to the shoreline and drift-fish. Keep moving until you find some activity and catch a couple of fish. Once you do, carefully and quietly

ease the anchor overboard so that you can stay in the fish-catching zone. Of course, when the action stops, pull anchor and start moving again.

7. No one particular pond will produce more than the others will—you'll need to scout out and find the ponds holding fish. You'll identify them right away because you'll actually be able to see the redfish. They'll either be pushing torpedo-like wakes ahead of them or they'll be clustered over one particular spot with their backs and tail fins out of the water.

One final note of caution—regardless of the time of year you fish (but particularly during the winter months), watch the weather and head back to the marina whenever squalls and thunderstorms threaten. No catch is worth the risk of being swamped or being struck by a bolt of lightning. I dissuade you from practicing that age-old "one more cast" thing. Most of the time you just won't have time for one more cast!

CHAPTER 14

I Tink I Kawt a Puddytat

As far as Tweetie Bird is concerned, anything that wears fur, has a passel of nose whiskers, and meows is . . . *a puddytat!* Fishermen, on the other hand, have a more difficult task when it comes to fingering fishable felines. 'Cuz, see . . .

You got your blue puddytats.

You got your channel puddytats!

You got your Opelousas or flathead puddytats.

And you got your gafftop puddytats!

All this I've covered thoroughly in a host of outdoor publications over the years. But it has been brought to my attention by the majority of my fine readers that I neglected to highlight one of the most prominent puddytats of all, obviously (as I have been accused) because I intended to hoard for myself alone all the pertinent, inside information relating to the catching of this phenomenal sports species.

Yep—I'm talking about *Arius felis,* alias tourist trout, alias sea puddytat, a.k.a. *hardhead catfish!*

I truly apologize, y'all. Being the consummate professional writer that I am, what with such a long tenure in scribing outdoor lore and legend, I knew you weren't to be duped. I knew that as hard as I tried, my lame attempt to cover up the "real puddytat," the fisherman's "most popular puddytat," wasn't about to be overlooked by such an astute readership! So with full embarrassment, I repeat—I truly apologize. And I will now share!

Herewith in the next 20 or so paragraphs I shall disclose everything I know—*everything I've ever learned*—about catching "the quarry of the saltwater realm," the hardhead catfish! And what a thrill it is, too, to have one of these piscatorial adversaries at the terminal end of your line.

Sure, there are those of you who've clouded your sportfishing interests with such boring and wasteful species as speckled trout and redfish and flounder and who just cannot fully appreciate how challenging it is to the mind as well as spirit to tie into a hardhead.

But let me see if I can paint you a proper picture.

First, you should know that hardhead fishermen are a very dedicated but secretive bunch. Few people are aware of their mystic organizations and their area chapters—membership is generally closed and new members are inducted only by sponsorship. In fact, very seldom does word of the locations of their meetings ever leak out to the public. This is where they share with each other—even though reluctantly—secret baits and new techniques to increase their catches.

Of course, no one I've met will ever admit to belonging to the hardhead clubs, because no one I've met ever admits to catching hardheads. They certainly won't ever admit to wanting to catch them. And I doubt that you'll ever find any verification of those poor souls who have succumbed to the addiction of catching them!

You'll see this for yourself quite often, say, when you observe a fellow fisherman in a boat next to yours. Did you ever notice how when he catches a trout or a red or a flounder or a snapper he screams and hollers and holds it up like Muffasa presenting Simba to the inhabitants of Pride Rock? But let him catch a hardhead! You're going to see him crouch down along the gunwale of the boat, bend over like Quasimodo hiding a wood carving, and quickly attempt to shake the fish off the hook (or worse yet, pretend to pound it senseless against the side of the boat!) before anyone notices and wants to emulate his prowess and the excitement of the catch!

I'm telling you, these are great fish. And hardhead addicts will say and do just about anything so that they don't have to share the sport or the species with their fellow sportsmen!

I've even known some who suggest that their hardhead catches are accidental, by feigning rejection and pretending to blaspheme the little fish when it inadvertently ends up on the hook. But don't be fooled by this pretense. All these guys are really doing is trying to dissuade any interest you might show in their precious little species. Let's face it—they don't want to share the excitement!

Did you ever notice how some fishermen never let you glance into their tackle boxes, so that there's hardly a chance of you seeing firsthand the kind of tackle you need to catch hardheads consistently? Oh, they'll show you their trout plastics and their bassin' topwaters and even their wet flies, but you ain't gonna see hardhead tackle so blatantly displayed!

Did you ever notice that these same fishermen will also never let you see the small bag of market shrimp they religiously stash under the crushed ice in the cooler? This is their prime hardhead bait. Chances are you'll never know they got it!

Did you ever notice that these same fishermen nervously lie that the fish flipper you discovered in their boat wasn't put there for hardheads but mistakenly left aboard by their son's friend Nigel when he used it for taking short-shank hooks out of the mouths of sheepshead? Yeah, right!

Well, I just happen to feel that the time for all this deceit is over. I believe that it's full-featured reports like this one that will give all fishermen an equal opportunity to enjoy even those species a select few might want to keep for themselves. So in that spirit, I propose:

1. That each and every one of you this weekend and every weekend hereafter leave at home the split-tail beetles and the plastic Cocahoes and the leadhead jigs that you used to use for trout and redfish.

2. That each and every one of you this weekend and every weekend hereafter instead bring along a bag full of single

drop leaders, hooks, and teardrop sinkers to be used exclusively for bottom-fishing.

3. That each and every one of you this weekend and every weekend from now on carry along as bait only market shrimp or Monterey squid that you will cut into small pieces and thread on your hooks.

4. That each and every one of you this weekend and every weekend from now on will aggressively return to the water all those overhyped speckled trout, redfish, flounder, sheepshead, drum, red snapper, and tuna and actively fill your Igloos to overflowing with hardheads of every size—from little finger-stickers to mammoth offshore mud suckers.

For the first time in a long time you will come to relish the challenge of the hardhead species—finding it where it lurks, tempting it to bite when it doesn't want to, finessing the subtlety of its digging and diving runs, and mastering the prowess of not losing it at the boat.

No longer should you allow another fisherman to coerce you into throwing your hardheads back. Proudly exclaim that "those days of not knowing are over!" Tell all your friends that catch-and-release be damned—you're gonna keep what you catch.

And allow me to suggest that you don't just take the occasional hardhead. Seek them out intentionally. Find their habitat! Fish those areas almost exclusively! Then ask other fishermen where they've located them, and encourage other fishermen to catch them with you!

I remember reading a significant piece of literature once by a great outdoor writer (I don't remember his name!) who said, "It is a far greater thing one does when he shares his hardhead catfish catches with his friends and neighbors!" If there really is any meaning to such philosophies, it might be something you want to pursue. Just think: a couple of ice chests *each weekend* filled with hardheads, all of them filleted with an electric knife and passed out to all the neighbors, where they'd be marinated in buttermilk and my very own

Frank Davis Cayenne Garlic Hot Sauce to pique the taste, then coated with my fish fry and deep fried! Mmm, think of the possibilities!

I mean, doesn't it have about the same irony as if Tweetie Bird were to sink a 4/0 Kahle hook into Sylvester's hindquarters from a line dangling from his little yellow cage and shout out . . . *"I tink I kawt a puddytat"?*

CHAPTER 15

Dey Ain't No Such Thing as a Cocahoe Minna

By late afternoon, the winds had increased to hurricane force. Like shingles on a rooftop, every wave that pounded the coastline ahead of the tidal surge stacked up the rising water in layers, covering the marsh grass under several feet of the brackish foam. And along with the incoming water came the sea life of the Gulf of Mexico, spreading out over landlocked bays, lagoons, duck ponds, tidal flats, pipeline canals, bayous, and shallow lakes.

Not until 20-something hours later did the water recede to the gulf, restoring the marshland to seminormalcy. And not until then could Leosine Alphonse make his way out of his camp on the marsh to the flooded "facility" out back with the moon on the door.

"Pooweee, Momma!" he shouted back to his wife, Clotilde, who followed him closely on the waterlogged boardwalk. "Dat storm done blew the whole building over! Ain't nuttin' left standing here but the seat-box!"

Leosine leaned over and peeked down into the hole. He broke out in a chuckle.

"Dat water done got some high, yeah, Clotilde," he said. "Looka dis! Dey got minnas in my ca-ca hole!"

"What kinda minnas dey got, Leosine?" his wife asked with profound interest.

"Hell, I don't know. I guess they're *caca-hole minnas!*"

No one can really confirm whether there was a Leosine and

a Clotilde, whether that conversation between them ever took place, whether the period in time was after a hurricane or just an unusually high tide, or even if that's how the little baitfish we use every March through December got its nickname. But we are certain that the term "Cocahoe minnow" is a nickname.

Because if you check marine biological records, what you and I and thousands of other fishermen use almost every weekend to catch trout and redfish are correctly identified as *killifish*. A. J. McClane in his *Fishing Encyclopedia*, H. Dickson Hoese and Richard H. Moore in their *Fishes of the Gulf of Mexico*, and Dr. Bob Shipp in his *Guide to Fishes of the Gulf* each makes reference to the hardy little baitfish.

In their books, the authors label what we call "Cocahoes" as fishes belonging to the Cyprinodontidae family, which is of interest to a scientist, maybe, but does little to impress a weekend angler. As far as we are concerned, it's better to call them by their various common names—bull minnows, mummichugs, and (if you're Cajun) "larje."

Biologically, though, they're all killifish and along the northern gulf coast we have a variety of species—striped or longnose killifish, gulf killifish, marsh or bayou killifish, diamond killifish, rainwater killifish, and saltmarsh topminnow. What's more, I'd venture to say that on any given fishing trip, you'll fish with at least a few of the species (since each species has little or no aversion to mingling with the others).

Let me give you a brief description of each one.

The *striped or longnose killifish* is a fairly large one with a longer snout than his cousins. He also sports some distinctive bars along his sides and has a rather subdued spot high on the last bar just ahead of his tail.

The *gulf killifish* is the most common "Cocahoe" we use for bait, but it's also the largest, sometimes reaching upwards of eight inches. Of course, as fishermen we prefer them graded, so that we end up with the two- to four-inch size.

The rest of the family is somewhat more rare.

The *marsh or bayou killifish* is usually a small member of the clan, generally less than three inches full grown. But it has the most beautiful coloration of all the fishes, especially between the sexes.

Maybe only once or twice during your fishing career have you baited up with the *diamond killifish*. His group members appear to be loners, traveling singly rather than in schools. But one or two of them do occasionally mix in with gulf killifish.

And should you ever reach down in the live well and come up with a Cocahoe that has a bright yellow caudal fin and a reddish-orange anal fin, then you've got a *rainwater killifish*.

The *saltmarsh topminnow* is another rare species but, like its diamond-banded cousin, does sometimes infiltrate another species' school.

Regardless, though, of which species you end up with, they're all hardy little guys, able to withstand rapidly changing temperatures (they flourished during the deep freeze several years back), salinities, oxygen levels, and turbidity. But by far their best attribute is their ability to wriggle like a spastic teenager at a Backstreet Boys rock concert while having a 3/0 Kahle hook threaded through their lips. Now that's a performance!

Dan Rainwater, who for the past 10 years has earned the title of "The Minnow Man" by catching and supplying thousands of live killifish seven days a week to bait liveries from Chauvin to Lafayette, says the peak season is from March to November.

"Actually, it all hinges on the fishing season," he explains. "Oh, they're here all year long, but they're only in real demand when the fisherman is hot and heavy into the trout and redfish. These days, for example, I keep a steady 20,000 fish in my tanks and deliver about 10,000 a day to marinas just in and around Terrebonne. That's a lot of bait!"

Rainwater, unlike many of his coastal Louisiana colleagues, uses 16x12x6 rectangular hardware cloth traps he makes himself to catch his killifish, strategically placing the rigs in trainaisses and moving them on the rise and fall of the tide.

"You got to run them every half-hour," he emphasizes.

"Folks think all we do is put the traps out in the morning and pick 'em up at night. Uh-uh! It doesn't work like that. If you don't stay with your traps—and I use about 15 of them—raccoons run off with them, the tide rises and you can't find them, or the tide falls and all your fish die. It's work to do it right!"

The going price in Southeast Louisiana for live killifish ranges anywhere from 10 cents to 21 cents apiece, which means that even though the little guys are tough, you still need to protect your investment if you're going to fish with live bait. Of course, with killifish (as opposed to baby croakers, say) that's not a very difficult thing to do. All that is required is a suitable supply of saltwater and a good aeration system in your live well.

"I recommend you take them out of the well one at a time with a bait net as you need them," Capt. John Aucoin, renowned fishing guide at Golden Meadow, preaches. "But don't ever leave a bunch of them trapped in the net mesh in the well after you select the one you want for the hook just to avoid having to scoop them up again when it's time to rebait. The fish you leave in the net will become stressed, and they won't give you that excited wriggling action you expect from using live bait."

One more thing—when you get ready to use them to fish, don't hook them too deeply into the head. The barb of the hook should only pierce their lips, and it should go through both upper and lower. This method allows the killifish to swim vigorously, providing the action that provokes strikes.

But let's get back to the whole thrust of this chapter! Maybe I've been hanging out with the Cajuns too long. Or maybe old pronunciations, like old habits, are hard to break. But *killifish?* As Leosine would certainly tell Clotilde, "Na, cher, you know dat don't sound right, no! When we after dem trouts, I jus' can't axe you to pass me no killifish!"

Tell you what! I'm with Leosine. As long as I'm fishing, there won't ever be any killifish in my ca-ca hole. There'll be "Cocahoe minnas!"

CHAPTER 16

Mullets: Food Fish or Fancy Feast?

In Southern Mississippi, the old-timers call them "Biloxi bacon." In Florida, they're the sought-after mainstay ingredient for a smoker party on the beach! And in certain parts of Europe they're even considered to be expensive, imported delicacies. But across most of Louisiana's coastline, the only specimens to make the menu are those destined to feed the fish, which is why the question rages on . . . "Mullets: Food Fish or Fancy Feast?"

It's nothing to stroll the sandy beaches between Biloxi Mississippi, and Tallahassee, Florida, and find folks out on weekends cooking fresh-caught mullet over hickory or mesquite on portable smokers. Because along this particular stretch of coastal real estate, the striped mullet—*Mugil cephalus*—isn't considered to be the "throw-back trash" it is in Louisiana, but rather a true culinary delicacy.

Sometimes scaled and gutted, sometimes simply gutted and left unscaled, mullets are usually cleaned under cool running water, quickly "brined" in salt water, and then hung on racks in a smoker to slow-cook to a flaky, nutty perfection. The whole fish are generally suspended on wires by either their heads or tails and basted periodically with either a sweet and sour sauce or a soy-based brush-on marinade.

Of course, the story is altogether different along the coastline of Louisiana!

Mullets are generally looked upon as an excellent food fish

in Florida, principally because of the influence of the sandy bottoms that they inhabit. But in the muddy waters over the muddy bottom of the western Gulf of Mexico, they take on a pungent oily taste and are rarely eaten. Make no mistake about it, though, they are quite edible! In fact, it's that same high oil content that makes them so very palatable when they're fresh.

But let's back up for a minute. It's no secret that in the Bayou State, mullets have a horrid reputation. I'm thinking it probably stems from way back when they garnered a particular nickname I can't pen here. The moniker was based on the fact that they frequently invaded the watery territory directly beneath outhouses on the marsh every time the tide rose and fell. It's that psychological bent that causes us to continue to look upon them as "food fish" rather than "fancy feast."

The excellent nutty-tasting flesh of this fish has yet to gain the acceptance that it truly deserves. Residents along the lower Louisiana coast have no problem throwing a cast net over the schools of surface-cruising fish, stashing the smaller "finger-size" ones into live wells to be later lip-hooked and hung under popping corks to tempt and taunt monster speckled trout and redfish. But to eat them? Not a chance!

Unlike other fish that swim the coastline of Louisiana, we know a lot about mullets. During the autumn months large schools leave the inland bays and head offshore to spawn. They begin their lives near mid- to outer-shelf surface waters, where actual spawning occurs. Young mullets start off eating tiny plants and animals, but as they grow up their diet changes to plants and detritus, foods that are high in cellulose. Mother Nature, though, has given them a unique organ to help them break down the tough cellulose plant walls and free up the nutrients for digestion. What organ? Would you believe a *gizzard*? The same food-grinding organ found in birds! The mullet is one of only a few fish that possess a gizzard.

Within six months of the large schools initially heading offshore, smaller schools begin to return to the bays and estuaries they left. The larvae and very young work their way shoreward and enter coastal waters at about an inch or so. During spring they grow rapidly and by summer they are cigar size, which is when they're most appreciated because that's when they become outstanding fish bait.

Mullets nearly always school up. From the smallest silver juveniles to the largest adults their numbers can be easily spotted near shore, in part because the schools are so near the surface. During those days in the estuaries, a number of maturing mullets always wanders well into fresh water. Some accounts have them occasionally caught by cast-netters more than a hundred miles upstream.

If Louisiana ever had a developing fishery for mullet for their flesh, it was inadvertently halted by the legislature some time back. What happened was the legislators recognized that mullets were really prized for their roe and a market indeed existed. So, presumably acting for the good of the species, the lawmakers restricted mullet harvest to the period between the third Monday in October and January 15 and outlawed harvest with any gear other than a strike gillnet.

As it turns out, that period during which the season is open is when mullet roe is mature and prime. However, it just so happens that that same time frame is also when the flesh is at anything but its best quality. Add to poor timing the fact that handling procedures for the roe fishery do not produce good food fish and you end up with mullet carcasses destined to be sold for cat food and crab bait.

The striped mullet is one of our most abundant fish, even more so than hardhead catfish! In late summer and early fall, they begin to form large, tight schools. Sometimes, they can be seen in knotlike balls with their heads actually protruding from the water's surface. These schools are most often near the lower estuaries and are a sure prelude to their offshore spawning run. This is also the time when big trout tend to feed voraciously on mullet. Ask the old-timers and they'll tell you, "See a big school of mullet swimming on the surface and you'll find a bunch of big trout swimming under them!"

Oh, here's a bit of trivia: *have you ever wondered why mullet jump?* The experts hint that there are lots of possible reasons. But in truth, nobody really knows. They can and will jump when alarmed, and they jump whenever they come onto a shallow bar or shoal. But no one has ever been able to explain scientifically why one mullet in a massive school suddenly decides to take a jump, and then maybe another and another, before resuming his place right back in the middle of the school. Hmmm— maybe it's one of those mysteries of the universe.

While on the subject of trivia, there is one other issue in need of address. You know that little fish we call the *channel mullet?* Well, stop calling it a mullet. Everybody calls it a mullet, but it's not a mullet at all. It's really a whiting and a member of the drum and redfish family. Of course, who can argue how good the fish is? Its flesh is firm and sweet and it freezes well. If you've never had them you probably won't find them at your favorite restaurant, because most are sold almost exclusively through retail seafood markets. On second thought, forget what I said— you can call it a *mullet* if you want!

Mullets are particularly vulnerable to gillnets and cast nets. They command the lowest price of any of the commercial fry-fish consumed by humans and in many areas create no demand at all. However, recent efforts to export mullet to Europe (especially Italy) and enhance its public image by changing its name to "lisa" have met with some success.

So let's suppose you decide to disregard all the psychological negatives and you want to know how to fix mullets for a "fancy feast"(not the cat food by the same name). Here's what you do:

• If you intend to fry them (and they're outstanding when fried right out of the water), fillet them, wash the fillets well under cold running water, dredge them in your favorite fish fry (I personally like the Frank Davis brand), and deep-fry them at 350 degrees until golden brown and crispy. I don't recommend frying, however, once the fish has been in the ice chest for over four hours. The heavy oils begin to build up!

• If you intend to grill or smoke them, either fillet or gut and draw them *(if you choose the latter make sure you remove every trace of mud from inside the belly cavity!)* and proceed from there. Filleted fish can be marinated in olive oil, sprinkled with seasonings, and grilled to à nutty perfection; whole fish can be marinated or soaked in a brine solution, hung in the smoker, basted with a honey-soy sauce-ginger mixture, and cooked until semidry, sweet, and flaky.

But that's it—don't stew 'em, cook 'em in courtbouillon, float 'em in an étouffée, smother 'em in a sauce piquante, none of that! They're too too oily!

So you see, in the end it's really up to you—*and only you*—whether mullets are "food fish" or "fancy feast." Personally, since I'm still having pretty good luck on Thursdays and weekends catching a few trout and reds, I'm going to think about it for a while!

Field Note: To use mullets for bait . . .

1. Use the small ones, called finger mullets, live. Simply hook them through the lips and work them under a popping cork on the surface or on a Carolina rig on the bottom.

2. Take the larger ones and turn them into what's called "cut bait." Freeze them or catch them and ice them down, then cut them crosswise into medallions about a half-inch thick. Then attach the pieces to a 4/0 Kahle hook, tie it onto a Carolina rig, and fish it on the bottom for reds, drum, flounder, and red snapper.

CHAPTER 17

Then the Gulf Turned Gold

"Hundreds upon hundreds of redfish, if not thousands upon thousands, suddenly rose to the surface, violently striking at anything floating on the water! It was like picking them out of an aquarium. . . . Then the Gulf Turned Gold!"

This is absolutely the very last time I'm going to tell this story. It's just too distressing to recall over and over again. I mean, once you get to thinking about it, you lose track of where you are and what you should be doing! It's like being transported to another dimension and time. Concentration is impossible! And the physical—you just can't control the physical. Your palms get sticky, your heart pounds inside your rib cage, your eyes get all glassy, and sweat just pours out of your body! I'm telling you, no one should ever have to recall such a moment over and over again. This is the last time—*the absolute last time*—I'm telling this story!

It was early in the morning, shortly after sunrise, maybe a half-dozen or so miles out of Tiger Pass at Venice. We were on Mike Frenette's *Lil' Teaser,* and all the night before and all morning since we gathered for pancakes and sausage in the clubhouse kitchen, Mike did nothing but boast of the pending phenomenon.

"I can't describe it!" he clamored, practically incoherently. "It's like something you only see once in a lifetime—only it's happened every day now for a week. Wait! Just you wait. It's gonna happen again today. You'll see!"

It was difficult to comprehend his exuberant speech, but we were semiready for it. Fortunately, a few of the dockhands at Cypress Cove Marina had forewarned my television crew that Frenette would possibly appear to talk gibberish at some point during the next day or so, something about schools of redfish rising to the surface and violently striking at anything floating on the water. But never mind. I had been around for a long time and I had been into schools of fish before. Never had any of them caused me to come unglued.

But I was soon to eat every one of those words.

"So where is this mass of redfish, Mike?" I asked my host, almost at the instant he shut down the twin outboards.

"Just be patient!" he answered. "You'll see 'em. And you'll know in advance when to get the camera ready!"

Much in the manner of a classic soothsayer from the pages of mythology, for the next 10 minutes Frenette explained in detail what was about to transpire. He said if the previous patterns repeated, the glassy Gulf of Mexico immediately adjacent to our boat would gradually begin to ripple, almost as though a gentle wind were gliding over the surface. Only it wouldn't be wind. It would be the first rise of some very small baitfish—rain minnows or such.

Then the "ripple" would become slightly more active—an occasional splash or a few frothy bubbles here and there where skipjacks would begin to amass under the minnows to surface-feed on them.

Then would come a rigorous feeding surge—large schools of skipjacks and hardtails up high in the water column, gorging themselves on the helpless minnows.

And then would come the seagulls, diving into the melee to pick up regurgitated fish pieces floating on the water above the initial attack.

"And then it happens!" Mike shouted excitedly. "All this other stuff has to happen first, kinda like a prelude to the performance. But then the big thing happens! Almost in a flash these huge schools of redfish—*I'm talking redfish that average 36 inches up to 47 inches!*—charge to the surface in a frenzy! And you don't dare dangle a line over the side for fear of some monster trying to rip your arms out of their sockets!"

Terry Jones, the ace veteran cameraman who up to that time had shot just about 99.9 percent of my television fishing shows for Channel 4, interrupted.

"Well, Mike, if they come up to the top like you're telling me they're gonna do, I'll get some video to end all fishing video!"

Frenette suddenly was distracted by something off in the distance. "Then you get that camera up on your shoulder, podnuh, 'cuz it's fixin' to go down!"

Terry and I both glanced in the direction Frenette was looking. Other fishermen aboard, who had been listening attentively to what he was explaining, suddenly stood up, leaned over the gunwale as well, and stared out at the now rippling water.

"Dem babies are here! Here they come!" Frenette shouted. "Get some lines ready!"

"What kinda bait?" one of the fishermen asked.

"Bait?" Frenette retorted. *"What bait?* Hell, they're so thick they'll hit plain hooks!"

At that moment, at about 15 minutes past 8 o'clock, everything Frenette had described came to fruition, almost as if the great hand of Mother Nature had scripted it. The gentle ripple turned into a moderate splash, the splash became a cluster of distinct swirls on the surface, the swirls turned into liquid turbulence, the turbulence became a rolling boil of flashing baitfish, and then the gulf turned gold!

"Get 'em! Get 'em! They're all around us!" the chants went up.

Almost immediately, all the fishermen aboard *Lil' Teaser* had lines in the water—some had shrimp pieces tipping the hooks, others had perfectly rigged plastic beetle tails, still others (as Frenette had suggested) had no bait at all. Within seconds of the hooks becoming submerged, every fishing rod was bent over double.

Now in the next couple of paragraphs I'm going to describe exactly what happened. But unless you actually saw the video we aired the night of the fishing trip, I wouldn't expect you to be able to fathom any of it.

For about 40 minutes—and that's all it lasted—everybody aboard *Lil' Teaser* caught fish after fish after fish nonstop. It was impossible to put a bait in the water, or even to dangle an empty hook over the side, without several big reds all at the same time striking at the same bait or the same hook! It was like fishing at one of those church carnival booths, where you take a dowel pin with a line and a coat-hanger hook tied to it and snag out little wooden fish as they float by.

Only these weren't wooden fish! These were monster red-fish, all over 30 inches long and many well over 47 inches. They were practically wall to wall, stacked thick in the water against each other in oval-shaped clusters within 30 to 40 yards of the boat. They were feeding voraciously and attacking whatever filtered down through the depths, ramming the sides and underbelly of *Lil' Teaser* in the onslaught. There was no such thing as having to cast! All you had to do was "dip" the hook overboard. In fact, the most difficult part of the entire experience was deciding which fish you wanted to catch—you could literally pick and choose!

There was near bedlam aboard the boat. We were each shouting and yelling and whooping and hollering. Dropping hooks over the side. Setting hooks before they were wet good. Tangling lines where two and three fish crossed over each other. Breaking monofilament where drags weren't set properly. Yanking played fish over the side. Hop-scotching over thrashing fish on the floor of the boat. Sorting and culling and catching and releasing.

And then they were gone!

The feeding frenzy stopped. The surface agitation quieted. The water where the school had been, beaten to a froth like a foamy head on a mug of beer, settled into a slick. Seagulls that had been diving relentlessly into the carnage for scraps all flew off to the edge of the horizon. We fishermen were left standing there with busted rod tips and frayed lines and damaged drags.

"That's it!" Frenette sighed in disappointment. "It's the same thing they did yesterday, and the day before that, and the day before that. They come up, they feed, and they're gone! We can only hope they'll come back tomorrow."

Biologists I queried about the phenomenon have little explanation to offer. Some say perhaps the bait schools concentrate following an unusually good spawn, likewise concentrating the schools of redfish. Others attempt to be more philosophical, supposing that the influence of the tidal surges in conjunction with barometric fluctuation affects magnetic orientation, stimulating all redfish within a given area to rush to mass feeding. And then you've got those few who agree that it only takes place when sunspots erupt in the nebula Ranzubia at the exact same time your mother-in-law clips her toenails.

But one thing is for certain. Only a handful of fishermen anywhere have ever been in the right place at the right time to see it all happen. So I figure it this way. I really don't have to know why it happens—I'm just happy I was there when it did! And that I got pictures to prove it!

Oh, wait, I nearly forgot. I promised to tell the members of the Old Codgers Club at the Sandfly Lodge about the redfish. I know—after I tell them then that will be the last time I tell the story. No, really!

Field Note: A few years back, about midway through the month of November, a similar occurrence took place for several days in Lake Pontchartrain. The individual fish weren't nearly as big as those we observed at Venice, but the schools were massive. Stay alert and watch the horizon—it could reoccur almost anytime!

CHAPTER 18

Draggin' and Snaggin'

Almost every day of the year you'll find anglers on the water at their favorite spots, catching fish on the bottom, by cast and retrieve, on the surface with a topwater bait, and even under a popping or rattling cork. But every year in midsummer, fishermen will tell you quickly that the best way to catch 'em is by "Draggin' and Snaggin'"!

It's plastic birds and frozen ballyhoo and prerigged baby bonito for tuna offshore. It's Coon-Pops for monster tarpon in West Delta. It's a No. 3 Drone Spoon for king mackerel at the sulfur mine off Grand Isle. It's the queen-size chartreuse and red split-tail beetle in the winding bayous just below Shell Beach. And it's Mirro-Lures and Rat-L-Traps for speckled trout all along the trestle in Lake Pontchartrain.

This is the "what, where, and what for" of summertime trolling in Southeast Louisiana, a method of sportfishing that is often given the slang term of "draggin' and snaggin'." And the experts will tell you that at times it is the only method that actually produces fish—*big fish!*

Let's look at the different tactics one by one.

Offshore—This is where plastic "birds" (devices that look like small model airplanes and that keep the natural baits "flying" near the surface) are pulled at about 900-1,100 rpm behind a moving boat to attract marlin, sailfish, tuna, wahoo, and other big game fish up to the surface. Veteran offshore trollers generally pull two "flat lines" directly behind the boat from the rod holders and two more "distance lines" off the outriggers. Each line is staggered, though, one at about 20 yards, another at 40 yards, and the two off the outriggers at 60 and 80 yards.

The baits are usually dragged high in the water column up near the surface, so that when the strike comes the fisherman usually sees it coming! The fish instinctively hits the bait, immediately darts off in a 90-degree direction from the initial movement, and the fight is on. More times than not, the fish hooks itself! I recommend that when you do big-game off-shore trolling you immediately get all the other lines out of the water once the first fish is hooked (this keeps line tangling to a minimum and reduces a large possibility of losing the fish to fouled monofilament).

Inshore/offshore for tarpon—Wherever fishermen go after sil-ver kings, especially in the West Delta area below Grand Isle and Empire, you can bet money that they'll be dragging Coon-Pops. Created and designed by South Louisiana tarpon veteran Lance Schouest, they've become the latest and most innovative artificial lures on the market for silver kings because they increase the catch vs. strike ratio.

Like general offshore trolling, four lines are typically set out in staggered fashion behind the boat—*two flat lines and two on outriggers*—and the Coon-Pops are pulled at about 700-900 rpm. Again, snapping the rod tip to set the hook when a fish strikes, as was required in the old days, is no longer neces-sary since the tarpon generally hook themselves.

No. 3 Drone Spoon for mackerel—Drone Spoons are usually trolled in much the same manner as Coon-Pops, with four lines behind the boat, but all of them are fished flat in the hands of the anglers instead of from rod holders and outriggers. Trolling speed varies depending upon tide and wave action, but usually it ranges somewhere between 600 and 900 rpm.

Spoons are ideally fished around structures—oil rigs, petro-leum platforms, sulfur mines, buoys, sunken wrecks, and wherever Spanish mackerel, king mackerel, wahoo, cobia, and other top-feeding predator fish lurk. Trolling spoons usually requires proficiency at the basics. You hold the rod, you feel the strike, you lock down the spool, and you set the hook. From that point on, it's you against the fish. And whoever makes the first mistake usually loses.

In this kind of trolling, it is also recommended that once a fish is on, the other anglers hurry to get their lines out of the water to avoid tangles.

Dragging the bayous below Shell Beach—The general rule of thumb is, "whenever you can't get trout and reds to bite by all the usual methods, drop the trolling motor over the front." Then on a seven-foot medium-heavy rod, tie on a full half-ounce leadhead jig, thread on a queen-size chartreuse beetle with the red tail, and begin dragging it behind the boat about 20 to 30 yards out. If you figure you're moving at "a normal walking pace," you're at the proper trolling speed. *(Note: The faster you pull, the higher the bait rides in the water; the slower you pull, the deeper the bait sinks.)*

Pay particular attention to sensations. You should be able to *feel* the leadhead "bounce and bump" off the bottom. You should be able to *see* the twitching in the rod tip. If this isn't the case, then you're probably trolling too fast. And expect the strike to come either as a powerful, distinct *bite* or a sudden *stop* (as if you just hung a snag).

At this point, set the hook and reel in your catch. Unlike offshore or big-game trolling, it is not necessary that other fishermen aboard the boat reel in their lines whenever a fellow angler gets a fish on. One pertinent suggestion, though: never horse a trout or red when you're doing this kind of trolling. Forward motion of the boat, pull of the tide, friction of the water, and force of the rod against the fish could easily cause you to lose your prize.

"Bayou trolling," which can be done at a lot more locations than just Shell Beach, can also be done with lures other than queen-size split-tail beetles. Magnum H&H Cocahoe tails, Super Grubs, Hybrids Flurrys, and even a wide variety of hard-plastic baits will produce significant catches. Lures should be tied directly to the monofilament (no leader, no swivel, no nothing!), and they should occasionally be "twitched" to dislodge any collecting grass or debris.

Trestle trolling—This has always been the hush-hush method by which the veteran anglers who fish Lake Pontchartrain consistently catch their "big trout." Here's how it's done.

1. Use either plain 20-pound-test monofilament or braided lead-core line to pull the baits.

2. Any good baitcasting reel will do, but all of the pros seem to prefer the Penn Level-Wind M9 or 209 with the adjustable ratchet.

3. A full half-ounce unpainted leadhead jig, fitted with either a Magnum H&H Cocahoe tail (avocado red flake, glow-in-the-dark, or chartreuse, preferably) or a red and chartreuse split-tail beetle, will generally produce consistent strikes. But again, if you ask the lake champions, they'll reluctantly tell you that nothing comes even remotely close to the blue and silver or the green and silver Rat-L-Trap or Mirro-Lure.

4. If there is more than one angler on the boat, have each angler hold his or her rod (as opposed to placing it in a rod holder). Stagger the distance at which each angler fishes behind the boat—one at 10 yards, another at 20, and yet another at 30 or even 40 yards. If you're fishing alone, then put out two or three lines (once again staggered), use Penn or Triton baitcasting reels, set the ratchet on open spool, and begin dragging. When the ratchet starts screaming, calmly pick up the rod and set the hook.

5. Fishermen use primarily two forms of locomotion when trolling Lake Pontchartrain—some use "trolling motors" at about midthrust; some use "outboards" at dead slow. It is still a point of contention as to which form is more effective, scientifically, since fishermen who use each style swear that their way is the best way. From where I sit, and based on years of experience, I suggest that each day on the water is different. I recommend that you vary your trolling speed depending on each day's conditions. Some days you may need to use the

outboard; other days the trolling motor will get the job done nicely.

6. In the lake, it is generally accepted that the best action and the best catches come from trolling the side from which the tide is flowing. In other words, if the tide is incoming, fish the eastern side of the trestle; if the tide is outgoing, switch over to the western side. By the way, most of the productive trolling in the lake is done on the *south end* either at the trestle, the Highway 11 Bridge, or the I-10 Twin Spans.

So now, when the big ones just won't bite on the bottom, or on the top, or under a popping cork, simply rerig, put the motor in gear, and try a little *"draggin' and snaggin'."*

CHAPTER 19

Wintertime Clusters

Cold-weather fishing has a unique set of circumstances. Trout and reds and flounder and bass occupy one habitat when it's hot and humid and an entirely different one when it's cold and dreary. But even more important, fish are easier to catch in spring and summer because they're scattered all over, but when it turns frigid, fish pile up in . . . "Wintertime Clusters"!

Amidst the drone of the clippers about three feet in front of me, the murmur of the college football play-by-play announcer on the TV set over my head, and the sudsy water being sucked down the hair-wash sink behind me in the waiting room, I could still manage to eavesdrop on a couple of guys in the barber shop Saturday afternoon discussing how important it was to have a trolling motor on the boat.

For a full 30 minutes or so they debated all the whys and wherefores—moving with the fish, covering a lot of water in a day's time, moving the boat without having to crank up the big engine, not having to subjectively pick a spot that probably wouldn't pay off anyway, not having to buy an anchor, not having to "pull" an anchor. I have no doubt the pseudoscientific explanations would be raging to this moment had the barber not ended it all with an impartial *"next!"*

Of course, you'd be pretty hard-pressed to find a fisherman who would not totally agree with the aforementioned reasons, but I also have to quickly add that none of them is the main reason for having a trolling motor—especially in wintertime.

113

See, in winter, your chances of just plain ol' coming up empty-handed are pretty darn good if your fishing rig is sans trolling motor. And here's why.

In spring and summer, game fish "scatter" throughout their highly adaptive habitat—one here, one there, one practically anywhere. And the axiom applies to almost every species of fish. Coastal marshes, beachfronts, rocky shorelines, oyster reefs, sandy flats, and open bays are all populated with an abundance of the spring shrimp crop, which translates to nothing more than a generous distribution of smorgasbord-type juvenile snacks and morsels attempting to grow to maturity in an almost perfect environment.

To oversimplify, virtually every cubic inch of water in the spring and summer will have something in it for fish to eat. And as far as fishermen are concerned, that means "just about everybody catches!" You don't have to know how to fish. You don't have to have the right boat or tackle or bait. You don't have to know any secret spots. You don't have to know any spots at all. Drag a bait anywhere through the water enough times during the day and it will be an oddity if you don't go home with something scaly and slimy and fishy smellin' to drop into hot grease!

But let's change seasons here for a minute. All of a sudden it's the dead of winter, and you've not only been dragging baits through the water, but you've cast every size and color of split-tail beetle and Sassy Grub and Mr. Wiffle in your tackle box so many times the plastic bodies are permanently bruised. And you still ain't found any fish!

Wanna know why? Because in wintertime the fish come in "clusters," which means you can fish all day long, end up in all the wrong places, and never even get a bite, let alone a fish! Winter condition—low turbidities, cold temperatures, decreased dissolved oxygen levels—causes aquatic species to crowd together, ball up, "cluster" in tight pods. No one really knows why. Maybe it's because the bait they feed on clusters in wintertime. All dem little Cocahoes ball up together, all dem shrimp ball up together, all dem baby croakers ball up together. So okay, this might not be the real reason, but we all agree that when you find the bait you find the fish, right?

Let me illustrate the perfect example. Some time ago my buddy Phil Robichaux and I were in Lafitte shooting speckled trout action for my fishing show. From about 6:30 in the morning until almost 12 o'clock . . . *nothing!* I know we had to have covered 25 miles trying to find any sign of fish; I mean, we were lucky to have picked up as much as a straggler trout here and there, and that was the two of us plus a cameraman fishing really hard.

Of course, Phil, being the consummate guide that he is, kept changing locations, kept trying new places, kept looking for that one key ingredient that makes for successful fish finding. He'd coast up to a spot then immediately drop in the trolling motor and turn it on.

"They could be *anywhere* along this shoreline," he explained, "but they're not going to be *all along* this shoreline. They're gonna be bunched up like grapes because we're in a wintertime mode—that makes them cluster tightly together in a ball. So we gotta find that ball, and until we do we're gonna cast and cast and cast and come up empty-handed. But when we find them, look out!"

The forecast couldn't have been more accurate had I been fishing with a fortuneteller. After we beat the water to a froth for most of the morning, Phil edged the boat alongside a broken grass island near Bay Round. It only took a few casts!

The fish appeared to be "ganged" in one little area between the broken part of the island and the main-marsh grassline. Every time the lure hit the water in that exact spot a trout attacked it! If we ventured off the exact spot, even by a foot or two, there was nothing—absolutely nothing.

Now don't think I'm talking only about speckled trout; true, speckled trout happened to be the species we were targeting that particular day for the television show. But in truth, this pattern of wintertime clusters works equally with redfish, sheepshead, drum, bass, and flounder too. Pick the right spot (or should I stay "stumble" onto the right spot) and you'll be into them big time! Choose the wrong spot, though, and you'll be out of them completely. There's no middle of the road. You'll either catch a ton of them or you won't catch a one! Which goes to prove that this is the time of year a trolling motor could very well be the most important piece of fishing equipment you could own if you plan to locate fish.

So all along the northern gulf coast from about mid-January until, say, Easter Sunday, here's the strategy you should use:

1. *Don't* anchor at every spot you pick (not unless you're telepathic and you can feel within your brainwaves full limits of fish in close proximity). Instead, coast to a likely location using the main outboard, do it quietly so as not to spook the fish in the shallow water, put in the trolling motor, and use it to scan the entire shoreline.

2. *Do,* however, place the anchor on the bow deck in the "ready" position, so that when you come up on a spot that instantly produces fish as fast as every fisherman on your boat can throw a lure, you can *ease the anchor over!* And that's where you stay, 'cuz that's the exact spot where you'll continue to catch fish until you get your limit.

And you will—in clusters!

CHAPTER 20

It's No Wonder You Don't Catch Any Fish

Use an inappropriate bait, anchor on the wrong side of the bayou, tie on totally unnecessary rigging, fish with too heavy a line and tackle, full-throttle up to a spot so that you throw a prop wash, which will scare everything off and erode half the marsh bank, and . . . "It's No Wonder You Don't Catch Any Fish"!

If you ever just drifted idly across some of Southeast Louisiana's most popular fishing spots and did nothing but watch how some fishermen fish, you'd see for yourself and you'd understand why I titled this chapter the way I did.

Many a morning out there on the marsh, I've felt sorry for the two guys anchored in the boat down from me, fishing 50 feet deep out in the center of the channel when all the fish were stacked up in 2 feet of water against the bank.

Many a morning out there on the marsh, I've felt sorry for the lone fisherman down the bayou who obviously had every conceivable lure in his tackle box except the one that virtually every single fish swimming that day wanted for breakfast.

Many a morning out there on the marsh, I've felt sorry for the man and his wife puttering up and down the canal—*ruining the fishing for everyone else!*—desperately looking for "the cut" his brother-in-law told them was holding some big speck-led trout three months ago.

Many a morning out there on the marsh, I've felt sorry for the cute little couple sitting on white buckets on the bank, flinging Kmart-Special Zebco 202s rigged with two-ounce

117

teardrop sinkers on double drop leaders fitted with tuna hooks out into the center of the canal in an attempt to catch the school trout popcorning on the surface.

And many a morning out there on the marsh, I've felt sorry for the little boy propped up on the bow, trying to catch sheepshead with his dad's old 7000 loaded with dry-rotted, memory-coiled, 120-pound-test line rigged with a 15/0 Aberdeen hook!

Oh—don't misunderstand me. There's nothing wrong with two guys in a boat, or fishing by yourself, or couples casting from the bank, or kids angling off the bow. But if your main objective is for fishing to be entertaining, productive, and rewarding, there are definitely some serious rules that have to be observed if you're going to catch enough to hold a fish fry! And after fishing—*and watching fishermen fish*—for all these years, I'm really not sure that everyone who fishes knows the rules by heart.

So I figure, hey, lemme see if I can help with this rules thing—maybe share with my fellow anglers a few set-in-stone, dyed-in-the-wool, never-to-be-broken tactics and techniques that in turn could help them come up with a bigger plate of fish and a whole lot fewer French fries. So with all due respect, here goes.

If, when you fish the bank for redfish, you pull up to the spot wide open with all 225 Yamaha horses churning up the bottom and pushing several mini-tsunamis into the bank grasses, *it's no wonder you don't catch any fish!* What I suggest you do to remedy the situation is, when you find a spot that you want to try, for example a spot where you suspect there are redfish holding tight to a shell bank or an oyster reef perhaps, cut the throttle on the outboard back to dead idle when you're about 30 yards away from the *actual spot* where you want to make the first cast. Then very slowly and very quietly *ease up* to where you want to start fishing. This way you won't spook the reds and you'll increase your chances of catching one on the very first cast!

If, when you drop anchor, you never ease it overboard but instead throw it with an impact equal to a depth charge detonating, *it's no wonder you don't catch any fish!* What you need to do, if you want to anchor properly, is slide the anchor into the water in such a manner that not even a ripple is created. Put it this way—if you can't hear the anchor go into the water, neither can the fish!

If you consistently insist on anchoring directly on top of the fish and then fishing where you should be anchoring, *it's no wonder you don't catch any fish!* Recently I putt-putted my 21-foot FishMaster from the main channel of the Rigolets to a grassy point just past the old lighthouse ruins. When I was about the distance of a good long cast off the shoreline, I quietly dropped anchor so that the stern would swing around in the direction of the bank. Next to me were about a half-dozen other boats anchored *on the bank*, their bows burrowed into the muck and grass.

Immediately I began casting, and immediately I began catching fish, hitting them at the exact spot where the bait dropped off the grassy shelf. It wasn't long before the guys in the other boats started to complain, asking how it was I could catch fish while they couldn't. The answer was simple: I hadn't anchored on top of the fish!

If you refuse to take along live Cocahoes or shrimp and refuse to fish with them when it's necessary just because Jimmy Houston or Bill Dance or one of them said once on TV that you never need to buy live bait because you can always catch fish with artificials, *it's no wonder you don't catch any fish!* Face the facts—sometimes the fish want live, real bait! And they won't give a second glance to anything artificial.

If, when you fish under the birds, you run the outboard directly through the flock instead of drifting quietly along with it, scattering the birds so badly that they abandon the school of fish they've been feeding over and you completely lose its location, *it's no wonder you don't catch any fish!*

If you insist on fishing with a reel the size of a trawl winch, strapped to a superheavy, offshore-style marlin rod that duplicates the rigidity of a flagpole when you're trying to catch half-pound school trout, *it's no wonder you don't catch any fish!*

If you always use snap swivels to connect your leadhead jigs and soft-plastic tails to the terminal end of the monofilament, *it's no wonder you don't catch any fish!* This is really an important point, because the unequivocal best way to get natural action out of soft-plastic baits and jig heads is to tie them directly to the mono with no hardware in between.

If you prefer to make wimpy little short casts instead of long ones when pursuing schools of game fish, *it's no wonder you don't catch any fish!* That's because if you can reach the fish you're fishing for with a short cast, then you're way too close to them and you're going to end up running all of them off!

If you intentionally use something like 50-pound-test monofilament when you're fishing for 2-pound speckled trout because you're afraid they're going to break your line, *it's no wonder you don't catch any fish!* There's no way you can feel the subtleties of the bites with line that heavy. Go lighter—15-pound test is a good all-around standard.

If you believe you can make all the noise you want to while you're fishing because your brother-in-law told you that it's not true that it bothers the fish, *it's no wonder you don't catch any fish!* Be quiet when you fish. And don't drop anchors, slam ice-chest lids, slide tackle boxes across the deck, and such as that—fish can hear every one of those grating sounds.

If you absolutely refuse to ever use light jig heads—like one-eighth and one-quarter and three-eighths—because you just can't cast light jig heads very far, *it's no wonder you don't catch any fish!* Try casting an open-face spinning rod for a while. It will get you a little extra distance with lighter lures.

If you don't know how to fancast, if you believe in your heart and soul that fish only bite when the tide is rising and falling, and if you don't have a trolling motor on your boat and don't believe it's necessary to have one to catch fish (or you have one but you really don't know why), *it's no wonder you don't catch any fish!*

But wait a minute. You knew all this stuff already, right? I mean, you only read this chapter for the fun of it, huh?

CHAPTER 21

Pipelines and Deadends

From about the time of the first winter cold front all the way past Mardi Gras, fishermen in Southeast Louisiana consider themselves to be in what's commonly referred to as the "winter pattern." Exactly what this means is uncertain to some, but to most it means that if you have any intention of consistently catching speckled trout and redfish, you had better be fishing the . . . "Pipelines and Deadends"!

Amongst those in the know, pipelines and deadends are very specific locations for catching fish during the cold winter months. It could be at Delacroix Island, Shell Beach, the Biloxi Marsh, Lower Barataria, Cocodrie, Golden Meadow, Leeville, Pointe a La Hache, or any of a hundred other locales in Southeast Louisiana—they each claim a large number of specialty waterways called pipelines and deadends.

For the record, these are almost always short-distanced, man-made canals that spur off a main channel somewhere. In all probability, petroleum companies initially dug them as service routes to their oil structures and wellheads. But along with the industrial progress came a secondary benefit.

Fish found the etched-out environment highly suitable to their survival, and it didn't take long after the dredging process was completed for these deepwater ditches, scattered profusely over prime productive marshland habitat, to begin holding lots and lots of fish, especially when the weather turned frigid. And then, of course, the inevitable happened—*fishermen figured it all out pretty quick!*

"When that first really cold front comes through I start fishing the pipelines," says Nathan Bourgeois, a veteran angler from Dulac. "And I fish *only* the pipelines until the last front comes through."

"It's where all our fish are in wintertime," charter-boat fishing guide John ("Hawkeye") Aucoin told me a while back at the Fourchon Boat Launch. "I know I can take my parties into the marsh on any given morning in winter, scout out a likely looking pipeline or deadend canal, and put them onto fish in a hurry."

"Those pipelines and deadends are the reason I venture all those wintertime trips across Lake Borgne to the Biloxi Marsh," Val McCormick admits, standing before his fellow members in his neighborhood fishing club. "I can practically guarantee myself, if not a full limit of reds and trout, a halfway-decent catch on a halfway-decent day. That's because pipelines and deadends have a history of holding cold-water fish!"

Novice anglers, however, should not be misled into thinking that all of this great wintertime fishing simply takes place without method or madness. You shouldn't go to thinking that every single pipeline or deadend you pull into will be the one where you load the boat. It simply doesn't work that way. There is no doubt that a degree of luck is involved, but there is certainly a whole lot more skill involved! For example, you gotta know the rules.

1. It is imperative that a deadend canal be considered a "closed system." This means it can be disturbed quite easily, and if it is approached incorrectly, whatever possibility there was of catching fish initially could be eradicated in a blink of the eye. Put more simply, if you disturb the water at the open end of a deadend, you can bet the ripple effect will advance down the bank and disturb the water (plus alert the fish to your presence) at the closed end of the deadend. What does this mean?

It means that when you select a deadend to fish, slowly and quietly drift into the canal and fish it (using a trolling motor or sculling paddle) from the front to the back. Do not run the outboard all the way to the back of the canal, then work your way out! You may as well drop a bomb in the water and use a bullhorn to tell the fish you're there and out to get them.

2. Pipelines and deadends should be fished ridiculously slow! Keep in mind that the fish are in there to find deeper water, which to them translates to warmer water (the deeper, the warmer). So since they are cold-blooded animals and will feel as though they've been in an ice slush in the Igloo when you haul them aboard, do you really think that these chilled and sluggish fish will aggressively pursue a fast-moving bait? Not on your life, they won't!

So it takes special strategy to get them to *bite* ("strike" is not a good winter-fishing word because cold fish don't really strike—they barely mouth the bait and you have to be ready for it). The experts all agree that you get them to bite by barely—*and I do mean barely*—moving the bait along the bottom. Wait! Let me belabor the point a little.

If I use the analogy of worming for bass, considering how very minutely you move the lure along the bottom, lifting the rod tip ever so slowly then taking up the slack with the reel on the retrieve, can you picture in your mind's eye just how slowly you should be fishing? Good! Fish pipelines and deadends just that slowly!

3. Never stay in one spot in any pipeline or deadend. Start on one end (the open end, remember!) and use the trolling motor or sculling paddle to allow you to fancast the entire shoreline length of the pipeline or deadend, up and down both banks and into the middle as well (in fact, particularly in the middle).

Once again, recall why trout and redfish retreat to pipelines and deadends in the first place—*deeper water means warmer water.* So the fish that you're searching out may show up along the shallow drop-offs at the shoreline only if and when the sun really warms the water. If it doesn't, those fish will stay deep, they'll barely move, and they'll do no more than mouth the bait so delicately you will have to concentrate intently to feel the bite. But that's wintertime fishing, at its finest!

4. Use *both* natural and artificial baits. Winter is the one time of year when fish become extremely temperamental. One day they could want only live Cocahoes. The next day they wouldn't take a Cocahoe if you begged them on bended knee! So how do you negotiate this? You give them exactly *what they want when they want it.*

Your most productive terminal tackle is going to be either a sliding-sinker Carolina rig with a Kahle hook (for your live Cocahoes) or a plain, unpainted, one-eighth- or one-quarter-ounce jig head fitted with the "plastic du jour" in which they take an interest. I'm suggesting a split-tail beetle in smoke-flake, glow-in-the-dark, white, salt and pepper, or clear sparkle, or an H&H Cocahoe in avocado, purple with a white tail, motor oil, or black with a chartreuse tail. Of course, they could very well want something entirely different!

When all is said and done, versatility definitely has to play a part in your winter fishing plans. You must feel comfortable using live bait. You must know how to present and work a variety of artificial baits. And you have to engage the elements and negotiate them via Mother Nature's rules.

Unfortunately, too many fishermen opt for the wintertime comfort zone, choosing to stash away the boat from December through March and staying hunkered down in front of a roaring fireplace. Now while there's nothing wrong with a crackling fire and some hot buttered rum on a blustery winter day, you should know that there is a lot of fishing to do when it's cold out. But more importantly, there are lots and lots of fish to be caught.

You just gotta know where! Can you say, "Pipelines and deadends"?

CHAPTER 22

Whenever You Take a Kid Fishin'

They don't want to be the stars of a television show! They don't want to impress all their friends! They don't want to break a state record! They just want to have fun and catch a fish—any kind of fish, any size fish will do! And that's what *you* have to keep in mind . . . "Whenever You Take a Kid Fishin'"!

I felt so sorry for the little guy that I wanted to leap out of my boat, race across the crest of the waves, and whack his schmuck daddy (or whoever it was) upside the head with a hardwood paddle! For the last 20 minutes that he had anchored next to me, the man had done nothing but critique and criticize and correct this little boy, much of it shouted in the manner of the Gestapo.

"That was a four-pound trout, son! I can't believe you jerked the line that way!

"Reel it hard! C'mon, reel it! Are you listening to me or what are you doing?

"I'm only gonna say it one more time—don't put that rod across the seat again!

"I don't believe you're so weak you let that redfish swim into the outboard and cut the line like that!"

It was one onslaught after the other, seemingly without letup. In the short time his boat was next to mine, the man—you notice I don't call him a fisherman, let alone a sportsman!—had faulted the little boy for just about every catastrophe in his life and blamed him for everything but the destruction of the World Trade Center Towers.

"That's it! You're never going fishing with me again!"

Finally, there it was: the only significant thing this sorry excuse for an adult had said all morning. And it prompted a loud response, which fortunately he heard, not only from me but from the fishermen in the boats next to me. *"Yes! Please do that little boy a favor! Don't take him again! Please!"*

It has always been said that fact is stranger than fiction. And believe me, I didn't use journalistic license here to set up some narrative for the sake of writing another chapter. This account *is* fact. It happened just as I portrayed it, verbatim, while a flotilla of boats fished white trout and croakers at the mouth of Bayou Liberty in Lake Pontchartrain.

Of course, I'm not so naive to think that this is the only place such an incident has happened! Or that this little boy is the only one it has ever happened to. It has been going on forever. But real fishermen (as well as all the child experts) will be among the first to tell you that this sort of thing is a perfect example of how *not* to act (or react) when you take children out fishing, especially if your end objective is to teach them to fish and to enjoy it.

With that in mind, then, it might be a good time to revisit the guidelines for recommended behavior when you are out on the water with your *little* fishin' buddies.

Whenever you take a kid fishin', first define the objectives! You are going out to fish, not to do brain surgery or redesign the O-rings for the space shuttle. The mood should be light, laid-back, and even happy-go-lucky. Leave all *your* pressures (as well as your short temper) at home! There should be no tension or negative stress. Nothing you do for the next four to six hours should be taken very seriously. That is what fishing is all about.

Then, *have fun!* That is what kids are all about. You are there to do nothing more than spend a day on the water together, pleasantly, looking to snag a fish or two. This is not a time to reprimand the little guy for low grades on his report card, not a time to have him repeat mantras about not teasing his sister, not a time to dump all the garbage from your job on his little mind. Simply share the companionship on his level—be *his* buddy. Talk about stuff he likes! And help him try and catch a few fish.

Whenever you take a kid fishin', exercise patience! Kids are not adults. God makes them with limitations built in, which means that they don't act or react as adults would under the same circumstances. *Great Expectations* may have been an appropriate title for a Charles Dickens book, but it just doesn't describe what you should have of kids on a fishing trip.

Consider both his physical and mental capability. For example, it borders on the inhumane to insist that a six-year-old finish a muscle-wrenching battle with a bull redfish in Whiskey Pass "just so he can tell Mom he did it!" Besides, if you know anything about kids you will know that a 12-inch redfish is just as impressive to them as a 47-inch brooder.

Recognize their attention spans. The most exhilarating tussle with a tarpon becomes of no consequence to a child once oxygen demand causes the first few muscles to start burning. You got to realize that they get tired quicker than you do, and their accomplishments need not be all that great. So at times like this say something affirmative and complimentary like, "Okay, you got him whupped now! Let Daddy give you a hand bringing this whopper to the boat!"

Get with their program. Feed them every time they tell you they are hungry (we all know they just love to root around in the ice chest!). And let them take sips out of their drinks every three minutes, because kids will tell you that they get bone-dry thirsty every three minutes when they are fishing. For that reason, I suggest bottled drinks with a screw cap—they are a lot easier to take in and out of the Igloo. And never scold them for biologically examining all the fish you have already iced down. It has always been a kid thing to de-slime fish!

Whatever you do, just grant kids the luxury of being kids and doing kid stuff. And if the stuff they do ends up turning into a snafu, practice forgiveness!

Whenever you take a kid fishin', avoid the classroom approach to personal instruction. Teach hands on, not by lecture. The boat is no place for Fishing 101.

And don't tell him how to do something—show him. A kid can absorb information like a sponge. And if he is shown properly, he sometimes surprisingly performs the task more efficiently than the teacher. Don't be harsh! Don't be critical! Don't be his competition! And don't point out his inadequacies. In fact, it is best if you don't say "don't" while you're out fishing!

Whenever you take a kid fishin', teach him to do as you do, not as you say. Always set the good example. If you curse because you lose a fish—remember, he's learning. If you pull up too close to another fisherman, disregarding courtesy—remember, he's learning. If you keep undersize fish or over-the-limit creels— remember, he's learning. Keep in mind that his principles for the rest of his life are being formed by what you teach him. You should be instilling the techniques of finding fish, reading the water, figuring out the tide, calculating the results of turbidity, and other such practical stuff. And of course, there is never anything wrong with just having a nice conversation.

Whenever you take a kid fishin', Hakuna Matata. Simba, the "Lion King," had it all figured out. It's not astrophysics! It's not brain surgery! It's fishing, just carefree fishing. If you don't catch a thing, you won't go hungry! Your neighbors won't run your family off the block. And Junior's friends won't ostracize him from the Scouts.

When you got a kid on the boat, everything is supposed to be *Hakuna Matata*. You don't care about size, you don't care about flubs, you don't take anything seriously. You, and the little guy with you, are there only to have a good time—not to save the world from starvation, not to change the trajectory of an asteroid, and not to predict the exact numbers in the Powerball drawing.

Whenever you take a kid fishin', be sure he fishes with quality tackle. It is not a matter of expensiveness. It is a matter of equipment that works, which in turn will addict him to the sport. Remember, a little kid is already at a physical disadvantage to begin with—why compound his handicap by giving him a busted-up contraption that didn't ever work for you? Make it hassle free, and he will have fun and want to come back over and over again. But even your guardian angel wouldn't fish with you twice if you gave him a crappy rod and reel!

And remember—you are fishing *with him* . . . he is not fishing *with you*. Get my drift, here? What *you* catch is insignificant. Make sure he catches! Put your tackle down completely if you have to. All of the attention should be on your little fishing buddy. And if you have more than one child aboard, I suggest you take along only one rod and reel for yourself (and that just for show, as a prop). Because if you are doing what you are supposed to be doing—and you are doing it right—between rigging corks, threading dead shrimp on Kahle hooks, untangling lines, making casts, and removing out-of-control casts from T-shirts and shorts, you're gonna be too danged busy to fish!

Whenever you take a kid fishin', if you hear him say phrases like "the next time," you know you have done it right. And that's the bottom line—*next-time philosophy*. Make no mistake about it; it is your responsibly to create an atmosphere that makes kids want a next time.

The best way to critique your performance as a teacher and host is to watch for a kid who suddenly loses all interest in fishing and makes the comment, "I'm not gonna fish right now!" When a kid says that, he really means *you have made me so uncomfortable or you have yelled at me so much or you have corrected me so repeatedly, I've decided that fishing sucks and I don't care if I ever fish again—especially with you! And what's more, hell will freeze over before you will ever get me to set foot back on this boat!*

But if the entire fishing trip is so much fun that the kid just can't wait to do it all again, then you got yourself an A+ in teaching a kid to fish. But more important than that, you got yourself a brand-new fishing buddy, probably for the rest of your life!

Field Note: Just for the record, I have written this entire chapter in reference to a "little boy." But the kid doesn't have to be a little boy to be a great fishing buddy. For the past 30 years, my favorite fishing buddies have been little girls. The only disadvantage is that they tend to outfish you!

CHAPTER 23

A Garfish Ab-duck-shun

All Priscilla knew for certain was that the Eden Isles canal in front of her house had been full of frolicking, waddling, baby ducks. But now there was only one left! What unexplained phenomenon was going on? Or worse yet, was there a culprit doing a dastardly deed? Was it . . . "A Garfish Ab-duck-shun"?!

Priscilla Pendergrast's fingers frantically punched in the numbers on her touch-tone phone.

"Emergency 9-1-1. How may I help you, please?" the voice on the answering end asked.

"Hi, this is Priscilla Pendergrast in Eden Isles. There are a whole bunch of little babies missing!" she wailed into the phone. "You got to send someone out—the police, the sheriff, the Wildlife and Fisheries, anybody—to come find them. The poor li'l darlings have got to be missing their mommas by now!"

"A multiple abduction, you say, ma'am," the operator's voice quivered. "My God! Please stay on the phone with me and give me a description of the little ones as accurately as you can." Desperation was beginning to manifest itself even in the operator's usually steadfast voice. "Where were these babies before you noticed they were gone?"

"They were swimming back and forth across the canal," Priscilla answered.

"What?" the operator shot back. "The babies were swimming?"

"Actually, they seem to have disappeared like one or two at a time over the past couple of days while they were swimming," Priscilla went on, oblivious to the operator's alarm. "And we know they didn't drown!"

"*What?* You mean to tell me that an abduction has been going on under your very noses and this is the first time it is being reported? And how do you know they haven't drowned?"

"Well, none of us, including all my neighbors, realized anything was wrong until this morning when we went outside to see them and throw them some bread!"

"Throw them *what?*" the operator asked, astounded. "You people fed these children bread every morning? What kinda neighborhood is this?"

"Children?" Priscilla snapped back. "What children? I'm not talking about children! I'm talking about baby ducks. We had us a whole canal full of precious little brown and yellow wild baby ducks and now they're gone! Lady, you need to get off the phone and send out whoever it is y'all send out to investigate ducknappings . . . hello? Operator? Hello, operator, can you hear me?"

So okay, maybe there really isn't a Priscilla and maybe there never has been such a call logged into the 9-1-1 system. But there surely could have been. And you can bet that almost everywhere that there's waterfront property, the owners wonder if someone is in fact sneaking in under the cover of darkness and quietly making off with all the newly hatched baby ducks that show up every fall to swim up and down the canals behind their mothers.

May I allay your fears. Sorry, Sherlock—I doubt that anyone is out there at night unscrupulously swiping your ducklings. Instead, it's a good chance that what you're noticing is a *garfish ab-duck-shun!*

These great big primitive fish that inhabit our freshwater lakes, bayous, creeks, streams, canals, lagoons, ponds, back-bays—and every place else they can stay wet—not only dine luxuriously on crabs and mullets but are equally fond of and feast on baby ducks. Consequently, many a waterfront family who has whiled away the evening hours watching ducklings swim past their docks can relate to the old adage, *"Now you see 'em, now you don't!"*

In fact, when H. Dickson Hoese and Richard H. Moore penned the chapter on the alligator gar for their textbook *Fishes of the Gulf of Mexico,* they couldn't get past the third sentence in the copy before they wrote, *"Have been found with crabs, mullets, and ducks in their stomachs."*

Now usually, when I write chapters for many of my books, virtually all of them have to do with the art of fishing—how to, where to, when to, and so forth. But one really doesn't think fishing when one thinks—or writes—about garfish. Yet, these creatures are amazingly interesting by their very physiology alone. For example, did you know . . .

1. Gars, along with sturgeons, are generally considered to be the most primitive of all the currently existing bony fish that swim in our waters?

2. Louisiana has four species of gars? The longnose gar, alligator gar, and spotted gar are true freshwater fish, but they have an unusually great tolerance for salt water. The fourth species, the shortnose gar, will live only in fresh water!

3. The alligator gar is the one with which we are most familiar? Louisiana Department of Wildlife and Fisheries researchers Harlan and Speaker back in 1956 said that these "gars afford but little pleasure to fishermen because they are almost impossible to catch," and "there is little or no commercial value in garfish." However, in the last couple of decades, the species has not only become important as a quarry of bowfishermen but also serves as a primary commercial food fish, upon which our famous Cajun "gar balls" recipe is based.

4. The roe (eggs) of all garfish are extremely toxic and should never ever be eaten under any circumstances?

5. The gar has what scientists call a "modified gas bladder"? This is an organ used in part for breathing air. Yes, Virginia,

like all fishes, gars do have *gills,* but whenever their environment stagnates and low oxygen conditions become prevalent, they begin to breathe air from the surface using their primitive "gas bladders" (which oddly enough function somewhat like *lungs*)!

6. Gars also have a unique scale structure? They're called ganoid scales, a prehistoric design that actually interlocks each scale with the next, making the musculature of the fish practically impenetrable to any and all predators. Since it's also very very difficult to break through these interlocking scales with an axe or a saw (you can forget your Mister Twister Filleting Knife, Jack!), those gar balls I just referred to are hard to come by.

7. At last account, the world-record alligator gar tipped the scale at 279 pounds and was caught in 1951 in Rio Grande, Texas, and the current Louisiana state record belongs to Jimmy L. Thompson for a 179-pound fish taken out of the Red River in May of 2001?

8. Sportfishermen who are determined to catch garfish for sport (or a record) generally fish them with noose-type terminal tackle that includes floral wire and frayed yellow nylon rope? A loop large enough for the gar to get its head through is formed with the floral wire. The wire, in turn, is used to hold the nylon-rope noose open. The entire rig is then suspended in the water under an oversized float (sometimes the lid of a Styrofoam ice chest), and it is ultimately attached to about 60-pound-test fighting monofilament coming off a heavy-duty baitcasting reel.

A medium-size croaker or bluegill is dangled inside (and close to the bottom of) the noose frays as bait. Then when the garfish strikes at the bait, his mass of teeth becomes entangled in the frayed nylon, the noose pulls shut, and the fight is on.

Oh, and no fair ever using baby ducks as lures! I got a hunch this would provoke a call to 9-1-1 from a lady named Priscilla!

CHAPTER 24

Flatfish Fever

Did you know that one little bitty ol' butter-broiled flounder served with French fries and a tossed salad at most seafood restaurants will cost you anywhere from $9.95 to $14.95 (the 95 cents covers the cost of the fries and the extra slice of tomato they add to your salad)?

And at a more upscale restaurant, say one in the New Orleans French Quarter, that same flounder will show up on your check at $19.95 to $24.95 (because here they're going to use seasoned fries and probably arrange them in a Picasso design on your plate)?

Knowing all that, then, don't you know how lucky you are to be reading this chapter? Because in the next few pages I'm going to tell you everything you need to know to go out and catch your own flounders.

But first, let's start with the biology!

Flounders in our corner of the world come in about two dozen species, belong to the family Bothidae, are colored or marked on one side and pure white on the other, have both eyes on one side of their bodies, and spend virtually all of their lives resting on the bottom looking upward toward the surface for a snack. But, would you believe, they don't start out that way?

As soon as baby flounders hatch out, it is almost impossible to tell them from all the other fish in the water—they look and swim like all the other fish. But then it's almost as if Mother Nature started fooling around.

In a strange, almost magical transformation, the baby flounder's head soon begins to contort and flatten out. Then, as if by mystic spell, the eye on its right side starts to migrate to its left side and scrunches up in that little vacant spot behind its nose and above its jaw line. Then to physiologically climax the weird transformation, the fish—which up to this point has been swimming vertically—rolls over on its side, begins swimming horizontally, and from that moment forward rests flat on its side on the water bottom whenever it isn't swimming.

Flounders are close relatives of several other families of flatfishes, among them the soles (which, incidentally, have their eyes on the right side of their heads—who knew?), the tonguefishes (which we usually only get to see in the pickin' boxes on a shrimp trawler), and, of course, the halibuts (those 300- and 400-pound flounder-looking fish they catch up in the waters of the cold North!).

Closer to home, though, on the piscatorial popularity chart are the spottail flounder, deepwater flounder, ocellated flounder, three-eye flounder, gulf flounder, broad flounder, spiny flounder, southern flounder, sash flounder, spotfin flounder, Mexican flounder, fringed flounder, shoal flounder, dusky flounder, and three of their kissing cousins called "whiffs." But as far as you and that restaurant that charges you $24.95 are concerned, the one flounder we're most interested in is the *southern flounder*.

It's not that we don't occasionally catch any of the others, but this fish is abundant from North Carolina, around Florida, all along the northern gulf coast, and over to Mexico. This is the largest of all the gulf flatfish, sometimes reaching almost three feet in length and weighing upward of 10 pounds.

It has the reputation of being a voracious predator, masterfully camouflaging itself on the muddy bottoms it so dearly loves until dinner comes along. Then, with flashfire speed and a savage set of razor-sharp teeth, it strikes out at its prey, rarely missing (a trait that alone endears it to sportfishermen).

Speaking of fishing, the most effective riggings are . . .

1. A live Cocahoe minnow on a Kahle hook tied directly to

the monofilament and weighted down lightly with a crimp sinker, or,

2. A piece of market bait placed on a 3/0 long-shank hook, tied to a 20-pound-test shock leader, attached to the main line by a swivel, and rigged under a sliding egg sinker.

You do have to stay alert to one thing while flounder fishing, and it's this: wherever you catch flounders you're going to catch stingrays! Exercise extreme caution with these fish—they pack a wallop in their venomous stingers! I recommend you don't even try to reclaim your hook . . . *just cut them off, hook and all!*

As far as where to go to catch 'em, it would take almost 10 full pages in this chapter to list all the "good" spots where flounders can be caught on a consistent basis. So if you're wondering if you can catch a mess of 'em at Shell Beach, Hopedale, Delacroix, Port Sulphur, Myrtle Grove, Happy Jack, the Rigolets, Venice, Pointe a La Hache, Empire, Golden Meadow, Leeville, the Fourchon, Lafitte, Lower Barataria, Grand Isle, and even Bayou Bienvenue . . . the answer for each of those spots is *yes!*

All you do is head out during the warm summer months (that's the period they love best!) and look for their congregation points—close to shore in shallow water around piers and pilings, at rock jetties, on beach slopes, over marsh-island mud flats, near oyster reefs, and at the mouths of bays. What you want to look for are places where they can set up *ambush,* where they can either hide behind grassy outcroppings or bury themselves deep into marshline pockets, where they patiently wait to dine on shrimp, crabs, minnows, croakers, squid, and—yes—even artificial baits (like the plastic avocado-colored Cocahoe, the smoke-glitter split-tail beetle, the Creme-Glo grub, and—*believe it or not*—the blue and black Scentipede bass worm!).

Now, whether you prefer to fish natural baits (and keep in mind that they will readily take them both dead and alive) or artificials, you can catch yourself a full limit of flounders (officially 10 per person) one of two ways:

1. by fishing under a popping or rattling cork, or
2. by fishing dead slow on the bottom.

Here's how the determination is made:

If the water along the shoreline where you're fishing is choppy (in other words, if you're on the windy shore), it's more productive to fish under a cork so that the bait is barely suspended off the bottom. On the other hand, if the water along the shoreline where you're fishing is slick (in other words, if you're on the lee shore), you'll catch all the flounders you can legally boat just by making a cast and retrieving the bait "dead slow" by twitching the rod tip.

Now all of this sounds exciting, but you should know that there is one downside for the fisherman when it comes to catching flounders, and that's the flounder's lack of stamina. Pod'nuh, the fish has none! Oh, maybe for about the first 10 seconds or so after he's hooked he'll fight . . . but then he gives up. And I mean he gives up totally! But never cite that as a reason to nonchalantly attempt to swing him over the gunwale. Mistake!

The veteran fisherman's rule of thumb is . . . *all flounders should be netted! Because over 50 percent of those that aren't usually shake off the hook and drop back overboard!*

So are these fish really worth $24.95 on the plate? I guess the answer to that question is . . . "it depends upon who owns the ice chest the flounders are in!"

If you don't catch your own flounders and you have to rely on the restaurateur to plate them up for you, they might not be worth $24.95 to you. But if you do catch your own, clean them yourself, pocket and stuff them with lump crabmeat, and then slow-bake them in a rich lemon-butter-wine sauce . . . ain't no way you can put a price on them!

Even the smaller ones, deheaded, scaled, gutted, cut cross-hatched diagonally on both sides, run through some of my spicy fish fry, and fried whole and crispy in a pan of hot peanut oil . . . I mean how much do you get for them?

See, to catch 'em, and to cook 'em, and to clean 'em—well, that causes flatfish fever! And whatever that cost is, it's worth it!

CHAPTER 25

Fishin' with the Live Stuff

Soft-plastic grubs and split-tail beetles, two-tone molded Cocahoe minnows, acrylic-hardened diving baits, shallow-running buck-tailed crank-baits, multicolored topwater lures, jigs with living-rubber skirts, scent-injected plastic worms and lizards—they'll all catch fish when conditions are right. But sometimes you just gotta go . . . "Fishin' with the Live Stuff"!

We all know those guys who avow to fishing only with artificials. "Why, I wouldn't have that stinky ol' dead market shrimp in my boat! And Lord help me if you ever catch me fishing with live bait! It's just not necessary!"

Well, sorry, Charlie! But in my opinion, sometimes it really is. Sometimes they won't give your cast a second glance if you ain't a-dangling a *live* Cocahoe, or a *live* croaker, or a *live* storm minnow, or a *live* shrimp, or a *live* pogey, or a *live* shiner, or a *live* crab off the barb of the hook. Oh, I know some of you won't agree with that, but I must respectfully disagree! Been there, done that, got an ice chest full!

It isn't a matter of whether to fish with live bait or not. It's more "what's the best *way* to fish with live bait if you're gonna do it?" I mean, don't you think that most people believe all you do is stick the hook into some convenient spot in whatever kind of live bait you happen to be using and that's that? Hmmm! Well, maybe in this chapter, I can help enlighten just a little! Pay careful attention:

Live shrimp—In our part of the country they come in two

kinds for fishing—browns and whites. The fish really don't care what color they are, just that they taste good (which, to most fish that eat them, they do). What the fish *do* care about, though, is how the fisherman presents them to them in the cast.

If you, as the fisherman, hook them wrong, you will, first, probably kill them (which means you will then be fishing with *dead* bait); secondly, you will get nowhere near the optimum degree of fish-attracting activity out of a bait that is supposed to be "alive and lively"; and thirdly, most fish will know right off the bat that what they see in front of them is anything but real and that you're just trying to trick them and catch them with the hook you stuck in that poor shrimp!

So having said that, *if you fish live shrimp on the bottom, either freeline or on a sliding sinker,* hook them through the base of the horn or through the second-to-last tail segment. This allows them their natural range of freedom and gives their movement a normal appearance (you've got to remember that shrimp travel across the bottom in a lightly prancing, fluid motion). *If, however, you fish the live shrimp under a popping or rattling cork,* hook it in the meaty portion of the back, in the first segment right behind the head, so that it dangles horizontally in the water column (you want the fish to see the shrimp as if it were swimming suspended). Under no circumstances should you hook it in the head or tail for cork fishing, because perfectly normal shrimp just do not bob up and down vertically right under the surface, head first or tail first! See how a lot of common sense fits in here?

Live croakers—The old-timers will tell you, "You won't catch as many trout with live croakers, but you sure will catch some big ol' trout!" And that's the reason for using live croakers instead of any kind of artificial that makes the same claim.

So how do you fish 'em? Almost the same as live shrimp, with one exception. If you fish them on the bottom, either freeline or under a sliding sinker, hook them through the lips from bottom to top. This allows them to swim freely, almost unhindered. If you fish them under a cork, though, hook them in the meaty portion of the back, just ahead of the dorsal fin, so that they again can swim freely. If you lip-hook croakers and fish them under a cork, they'll bob vertically in the water column, which is a completely unnatural position for a swimming croaker—and fish that feed on him know it!

So what's the main difference between croakers and live shrimp? *The way you make a hook-set!* As soon as a trout takes off with a live shrimp you can set the hook, and most of the time you'll put him in the boat. But when fishing a croaker, top or bottom, you need to give a feeding fish more time to swallow it. Don't set the hook until the trout has almost pulled the rod out of your hand! Remember, he's got to strike, turn the croaker in his mouth, and get it down head-first. If you set the hook too soon, you pull the entire rig out of his mouth!

Pogeys—These live baits also take ultrabig speckled trout at certain times of the year, and for the most part you can fish them the same way you fish live croakers. In Southeast Louisiana, most pogey fishermen going after trout freeline them.

Here's a Frank Davis Fishing Secret—instead of using a cast net to catch pogeys, take an ultralight rod and reel rigged with eight-pound-test monofilament line and tie on about 10 drop leaders, each one fitted with tiny gold perch hooks, and a large split shot at the end of the rigging. Then cast out (hooks unbaited) into a school of pogeys and begin a rapid retrieve. The pogeys will strike at the gold hooks, thinking they're small marine worms they sometimes feed on, thereby snagging themselves in the process.

So what's the advantage of catching them this way as opposed to with a cast net? You eliminate stress this way, they're not so agitated when you put them in the live well, they don't secrete as much uric acid, and they stay alive 10 times longer. Give it a try!

Cocahoe minnows—While from Lake Charles to the Louisiana marsh we prefer to call them Cocahoes, they're really (and scientifically) killifish or mummichugs. In our quadrant of Louisiana we usually fish with both the longnose and gulf varieties, the gulf variety being the most common and the longnose being recognized by the vertical black bars it sometimes displays. The easiest and hardiest of the live baits there are to use, they should be hooked through the lips and tossed out into the current, whether you're fishing top, bottom, or cast and retrieve. Amen!

Finger mullets—Usually only a small contingent of Louisiana fishermen regularly uses finger mullets and these folks almost always catch their own. However, they are a popular bait with Breton Sound fishermen who seasonally surf-fish the Chandeleur Islands.

Finger mullets are just what the name implies: very small, immature, common mullets that are taken with cast nets, culled for size, and used to catch speckled trout and large redfish. They are not as hardy as Cocahoes but usually are hooked through the lips and fished Carolina rigged on the bottom.

Live crabs—These guys are used almost exclusively for catching bull redfish in the whitewater breakers along the beaches in Timbalier and Terrebonne bays. Fishermen usually search out the grassy shorelines in the marsh and scoop up both small and large crabs, which are then Kahle-hooked "live" through the base of the back flipper and fished Carolina rig, right on the bottom. The only other species fished with crab are bull drum, but the crab is usually broken into pieces before being threaded onto the hook (thus the terminology "cracked crab").

Storm minnows—Their real name is "fat sleepers," scientifically *Dormitator maculatus,* and the only time we really get to fish with them is usually right before and right after a major storm (which is why a lot of the old-timers refer to them as hurricane minnows).

When Dr. Bob Shipp wrote about them in his *Guide to Fishes of the Gulf of Mexico,* he said they live on or in the bottom, nearly immobile, blending well with their muddy or sandy surroundings, only occasionally peeking up at the world above them with their little beady eyes. As fishermen, we get to use them for bait only when the rough surf and tidal surge of a tropical storm or hurricane interrupt their restful existence.

They make a great live bait, are relatively hardy, and are obviously a delicacy to predatory game fish. In fact, my old friend Kenny Campo calls them "fish candy." But unfortunately, we get to utilize them only for a short period of time, because when the storm is gone . . . so are the storm minnows!

Now there are also some of us who, on occasion, use such critters as *flat sardine shiners* (those are the silvery ones you sometimes catch in your cast net), *silverside shiners* (those are the ones you see in the water at night under the lights off your pier), *pinfish* (those are the little bait stealers you sometimes catch while bottom-fishing), and even *hardhead catfish* for live bait (hardheads with their spines cut off are a prime taste treat for cobia).

While most avid fishermen would prefer to rig a quarter-ounce jig head and throw the ol' reliable H&H smoke glitter or avocado Cocahoe or the white split-tail beetle or the Mister Twister grub when given half a chance, these very same dedicated and mostly veteran anglers, when they get semi-desperate, and when their favorite artificials just ain't workin' all that well, will also confess that sometimes—*sometimes!*—you just have to start "fishin' with the live stuff."

Field Note: Just for the record, the correct name for the cigar minnow that we often fish with offshore for snapper is "round scad." It's a member of the jack family.

CHAPTER 26

Fishin' the Ditches—Leeville to Grand Isle

From the moment you cross over the Leeville Bridge to the second you set foot on Grand Isle itself, the 25 miles of southbound marsh and ditch paralleling both sides of Highway 1 are slap rotten with fish! And all you do is stand on the shoulder of the road, cast, and keep count of your limit! But you gotta know where to stand.

"So who the hell ever said you had to have a boat to enjoy a fishin' trip?" Reggie Naquin interrupted, butting into the argument between the two guys on barstools next to him. He just couldn't sit there, sip his beer, and listen to anyone ever make that statement again.

"I don't have a boat!" Reggie fussed. "Hadn't had one since Hurricane Juan took it off someplace. And probably won't buy another one anytime soon. But I want you two guys to know that I *do* have a freezer full of trout and redfish fillets, to say nothing of the sheepshead and the drum and the flounders I got stacked like cordwood. And I caught every single one of 'em fishin' right off the blacktop between Leeville and Grand Isle!"

Reggie isn't alone when it comes to fishing the Highway 1 roadside. Lots of his friends *fish the ditches* . . . and they *catch* fish every time they do. But you'd have to drive bamboo splinters under his fingernails to get Reggie (or any of his roadside fishing buddies) to tell you how they manage to take limits consistently alongside the ditches en route to "the island." To them, this is as much a guarded secret as are the numbers on an offshore rig where boat fishermen go to catch 25-pound red snappers. See, Reggie and his cohorts figure that if everybody who doesn't own a boat suddenly lined up along the highway between Leeville and Grand Isle, there'd be so many fishermen packed shoulder to shoulder along the shoulder, even the tide wouldn't be able to get in and out!

Fortunately, though, that's why you've got me! Reggie won't tell you where to fish, how to fish, when to fish, and what to fish with—but I will! It's my job as the author of this book! It's what you count on me to do. And you don't need bamboo splinters.

Just as for the guys who go out fishing from a boat, the secrets are *tactics, location,* and *techniques.*

Tactics—The first thing you want to do is forget that you're fishing off the road. Forget that you don't have a boat. The fish don't know any of that. In fact, if you're a good fisherman, the fish aren't even supposed to know you're there (wherever there is).

So as far as you're concerned, you're on a quest to place yourself in a position to catch fish . . . which means you first have to find a body of water that will support a fish population. Since you don't have a boat that you can run around in and scout out various areas, you have to come up with an alternative, land-based, fish-holding spot.

Which means it has to provide good habitat.

Which means it must have a source of oxygen-rich water of the proper salinity and clarity to support at least one primary species.

Which means it must also have "cover" so that it is capable of hiding the fish it supports.

Which means it must also have a good food supply nearby so that all the fish in population don't starve to death waiting for you to come along and feed them.

At this point, you're probably thinking, "Hey, wait! I don't see a whole lot of difference here between the roadside fisherman and the sportsboat fisherman!" Right!

If those are the requirements and prerequisites, you can rule out fishing in the 17th Street Canal, you can completely forget the swamp overflows off the I-10 system, and there's no sense in even trying the urban diversion channels.

What's more, the place you select must have good accessibility. You gotta be able to pull up alongside the spot, get out of your car (without being creamed by any oncoming traffic or getting clipped by some pickup-truck mirror), and cast to these productive areas.

Think! Think!

You gotta pick an area where there's every reason in the world to have a fish. It's gotta be directly connected to a fish-producing lake, bay, bayou, canal, pond, or slough. And to qualify as one of the most absolutely perfect spots, it should have direct tidal influence.

Well, bingo already!

The "road"—that long stretch of highway—between Leeville and Grand Isle fits the bill beautifully. It's great marshland habitat. Traffic is rather light most of the time. Water (the fishing area) abuts the shoulder. You don't have to cast across 15 yards of marsh grass to get the bait to the fish and then pull whatever fish you catch back across 15 yards of vegetation. What's more, the water in these ditches is calm, clean, and moving.

Like long probing fingers, the ditches branch off the Gulf of Mexico and its adjacent bays, which means that whatever tide affects the fish in the gulf will also affect the fish in the ditches. And if all that weren't enough, every place you look there are baitfish being chased! And on top of that, it's the least crowded 25 miles you've ever seen!

Right about now your heart rate should have increased considerably. *Because without a doubt, this terrain will hold fish!*

Location—Let's see how I can put it. Okay, you've found the ballpark. Now all you have to do is locate the entrance gates. And that's why "location" is the next thing you have to determine.

Not every spot along that 25-mile stretch will be a fish producer, so you could spend a lot of time indiscriminately "trying and sampling, stopping and testing" at spots along the highway. Of course, if you have a few months off, or if you're retired and your wife isn't hounding you to take her on a trip to the Smokies, you can conceivably test and sample to your heart's content. But really, who's got time for that? Most of us just want to make three casts tops and begin filling the Igloo.

So here's the deal. You begin to study the possibilities.

Out of this entire 25 miles from Leeville to Grand Isle, which spot should the fish be holding in?

Out of this entire 25 miles from Leeville to Grand Isle, which spot has obviously been overfished because it was too easy to get to?

Out of this entire 25 miles from Leeville to Grand Isle, what biological laws apply?

Well, whether in the Gulf of Mexico, Bayou Perot at Lafitte, Catfish Lake in Golden Meadow, Dulutts Canal at Shell Beach, or the Sulphur Mine at Cocodrie, the same conditions that govern fish activity and movement in those places govern the activity and movement alongside Highway 1. You gotta remember, that highway habitat is always correctly labeled *"borrowed bayou."* In other words, the state (and perhaps the federal government) borrowed dirt it excavated from the ditches to build the elevated roadbed a long time ago—which is how Highway 1 got there in the first place! So what you have to do to pick a productive spot is to find an area that has "been affected and influenced by Mother Nature." You want to avoid fishing the little straight-edge expanses along the road. In other words, if the section you're perusing appears to have the classic "ditch" look, keep on moving. What you're scouting for are sections where the ditch leeches back into a cut in the marsh, a drain opening in the grass, a man-made trainaisse, a tidal eat-out, a naturally eroded slough, or any other place where the tide can push gulf water onto the marsh or, conversely, drain marsh water southward to the gulf.

What happens at these spots (which happens nowhere else along the 25-mile stretch) is that all the criteria come together. The predatory fish—trout, redfish, drum, flounder—hide in the cuts themselves (as opposed to lying suspended in the ditch proper) and feed on baitfish flushed into and out of the marsh by tidal movement.

Techniques—So what does all this mean to you? It means that now, finally, you can apply the techniques! And here's how it's done.

You want to drive the road until you target such lacerations in the marshland. You then want to pull off to the side of the road (well out of traffic) and quietly watch for a minute or two. You're looking for bait movement. You're looking for predatory feeding activity. You're looking for wading birds giving away the presence of frightened fish. These are the places you fish! These are the places you look for. These are the only places where you'll catch anything consistently.

If you notice none of the "signs" and all the criteria appear negative, then, as they say in *The Wiz*, you ease on down the road for another half-block, or a block, or at least to the next eat-out in the marsh. On the other hand, once you find positive signs, quickly get out of the car, rig the bait you're most proficient with, and make your casts—first close to the bank, then farther into the cut with each succeeding presentation.

Redfish will be your primary quarry, with sheepshead, drum, and flounder coming in a close second. It's also not impossible to pull in a trout or two, but don't expect them to be as prolific as they'd be if you were casting open water in an open-bay boat.

Incidentally, while artificials will catch "clustered" fish from the Highway 1 roadside, it is my humble opinion that, to virtually guarantee success (to say nothing of muscle-wrenching strikes), nothing beats a live shrimp or Cocahoe minnow swimming frantically on the end of a Kahle hook. I also suggest you have one rod and reel Carolina rigged for bottom-fishing and a second one rigged for popping-cork fishing.

Traditionally, year in and year out, the best action has always been early in the morning and late in the evening. Of course, precise fishing times vary, as do the movements and times of the tides.

A few sidebar notes are in order, I think. Because you're fishing where a landing net probably won't be feasible, you might want to use a seven-foot, heavy-action rod that's been loaded with big-game-type line for Highway 1 fishing. There will no doubt be instances where you have to winch in a bunch of the big ones you catch. Oh, yes—you will catch fish!

A good pair of Polaroid sunglasses makes a big difference in spotting fish lying in the ditches and sloughs. I suggest you wear them whenever possible.

You've always been told to concentrate on fishing while you're fishing. Well, in this instance, you also have to concentrate on the highway. Don't get so preoccupied that you back out onto the roadway into oncoming traffic. And by all means, if you take your children fishing with you, watch them like a hawk every single minute. Remind them that they're fishing off the shoulder of a federal highway and that safety is of the utmost importance.

Finally, it's a long stretch between Leeville and Grand Isle. Bring along all the equipment you'd take with you on any serious fishing trip—ice chest, drinks, sandwiches, sunscreen, folding chairs, and so forth. You don't want to leave a good spot and drive 20 miles just to get little thirsty Junior a root beer.

And besides, if you don't stake out and claim a good spot once you find it, remember that it'll only be a few minutes before Reggie and his buddies show up!

CHAPTER 27

Your Brud-in-Law Knows
All about Boats

Ya got ya tri-hulls, ya got ya runabouts, ya got ya lake skiffs, ya got what dey call dem open-fishermen-bay kinda deals, and ya even got dem cabin-cruisers if ya was to go like deep-sea fishing and stuff. But ya don't got to go and learn none of that because "Your Brud-in-Law Knows All about Boats"!

It was almost terrifying. He looked the poor guy squarely in the eye, snorted a time or two, handed him a cup of the freshly tapped beer, and exclaimed so loudly that practically everyone standing on the floor of the Superdome could hear!

"I'm gonna tell you one more time—forget what all these nickel-and-dime sales guys are promising you. They're just out for the bucks! They don't love ya like family. You wanna buy a boat, you ask me about a boat! I did a lot of reading up on boats in my day. Boats is like second nature to me—little boats, big boats, sailboats, any kinda boats! I'm telling you, your brud-in-law knows all about boats!"

Stand anywhere within earshot of any of the brewski booths during the annual Boat Show and you'll hear this kind of oratory nightly. Never mind what the manufacturer reps say. Never mind what the mechanics for the dealerships explain. Never mind what the continuous-run videos depict on the 10-foot-high screens. The bottom line is *when it comes to boats, t'ain't no expert like brud-in-law!*

You've heard all this rap before, though, haven't you? Probably fell sucker to it once or twice during your tender years, when you just couldn't bear to tell your young bride that her egotistical, over-testosteroned older sibling might not know all that he professed.

Tell you what. If you cross your heart and promise never ever to mention it to "brud-in-law," I'll share with you what I've managed to discern from bona-fide boating authorities over the past 40-plus years of boat shows, dating back to the time when Lou Soroe, who first conceived the idea of a New Orleans Boat Show, was a teenager!

1. Never let someone else—that includes your wife, your children, your mother, your boss, your brother (and especially your wife's brother!)—choose a boat for you. You got to choose your own! You got to pick it out yourself, and don't let any comment here or there persuade you otherwise.

2. Never choose a boat because the colors match your Suburban, or your Labrador's eyes, or your spouse's new living-room drapes! Pin-striped, pastel-shaded gunwales, a taffeta-covered console bench seat, and Scotchgarded Teflon carpeting won't catch you the first largemouth bass, nor will they keep the seas from breaking over the bowrail the first time you run the dingy you bought out to the bluewater rip.

3. Don't buy a boat because your neighbor has one like it, or your boss has one like it, or a guy at work has one like it! You got to like it. And above all else, it's got to do the job you want it to do! I heard a guy one year at the boat show tell his companion, probably just a drinking buddy (who at the time had drunk a little too much), "Man, get the big one—you can afford it!" Well, he probably could have afforded it, but if the fact of the matter was he spent most of his time chasing marsh bass back in the duck ponds, why would he want to invest in a 40-foot MosesCraft that takes six feet of water just to float? Buy the boat that will serve your needs.

4. Which brings up another point—*there isn't any such thing as an "all-purpose boat."* There's all-purpose flour, all-purpose cleaners, and all-purpose seasoning, but not all-purpose boats. So when you buy your boat, buy one designed specifically for

the use you intend—bass fishing, marlin fishing, crawfishing, water skiing, Sunday barbecuing and drinkin', operating an independent ferry, whatever. But try not to stop someone at the boat show and ask where the "all-purpose rigs" are!

5. I also suggest that you don't buy a boat just because the dealer at the boat show bitched and moaned on the final day that he really didn't want to have to trailer all the rigs he hauled into the Superdome back to St. Bernard, and if you bought it at the show he'd knock off $20 and throw in a free anchor. I can promise you that you're gonna hate this boat the rest of your life! The boat you really want is the one you long to rush home to after work, the one you want to spend time on the weekends with (even if it's only in the garage), the one your wife is jealous of because you keep referring to it as your sweetheart, the one you never had second thoughts about from the get-go, the one that was love at first sight! Over the years, guys have told me there really are boats like this!

6. But you'll find them at a boat show only if you stay "beer free." Stagger one too many times to "the taps" while deciding between Rig A and Rig B and I'll guarantee you that the "jon-boat" you bought to scull around Pearl River in will be the size of the *Andrea Doria,* and you've also signed a promissory note to take delivery this weekend on the old Chalmette ferry that your brud-in-law suggested was a great deal as a second rig!

But, hey—wait a minute. That's right! Your brud-in-law knows all about boats, huh!

CHAPTER 28

Cats (but Not the Musical)

They don't purr.

They don't meow.

They don't come when you call, "Here, kitty, kitty."

They don't snuggle up overnight on your sofa to shed hair and cough up fur balls.

And depending upon which variety you end up with, you either love 'em to pieces or you curse 'em as the pestilence they can become.

I'm talking about one of the most loved/hated fish in the water. I'm talking about *catfish!*

The biology boys say they belong to the scientific family Ictaluridae. And if you think they only come in two models, check this out. You got blue cats, black bullheads, yellow bull-heads, common bullheads (also classified as brown bullheads or yellow catfish), channel cats, black madtoms, tadpole mad-toms, speckled madtoms, brindle madtoms, frecklebelly mad-toms, freckled madtoms, brown madtoms, mudcats, flathead cats (which are also known as tabby cats or Opelousas cats), seacats (best known as hardheads), and gafftopsail cats.

In the Amazon there are hundreds and hundreds of species, but here in Louisiana we are concerned primarily with about a half-dozen of them—blue cats, bullhead cats, channel cats, tabby cats, gafftop cats, and dem ever-popular, darlin' li'l hardhead cats!

Dan Noble, an old friend of mine who fishes regularly down in Des Allemands, the catfish capital of Louisiana, told me one time, "These are the sportin' models, the eatin' models. God made all them other ones so that the scientists would have some fish they could study." It's oversimplification, I know, but it's awfully accurate.

THE FRESHWATER SPECIES

The species found in fresh water make up the entrees for our table. At the top of this menu is the *channel cat*. It doesn't grow as big as its *blue cat* cousin (which is considered to be the largest of all North American catfish, some tipping the scales at 150 pounds and better), but it is much more popular with the sportsman. Then, too, in recent years it has become the species that commercial operators use most often when they want to privately stock, pond raise, and sell. Channel cats and blue cats are also the species most often caught in the wild by sportsmen and commercial catfishermen.

Of course, it's true that anyone who has ever been a fisherman for more than about a week will have boated a few species of *bullheads*—that's because they're plentiful in turbid ponds and bayous in Louisiana. Undisputedly, they're good eating, but they don't get the rave reviews the channels and blues get because they run so much smaller in size.

And it goes without saying that no Louisiana fisherman in his right mind would ever catch and release a *tabby cat*—the famed Opelousas or flathead, as we prefer to label him. Often reaching weights of 100 pounds or more, this clumsy but powerful aquatic giant can stop the heart of the most seasoned catfish veteran when it rises up to the surface for the first time during a fight. Bring home a big Opelousas and you feed the entire neighborhood!

For the most part, though, the heavyweight blue cats and the six- to eight-pound channel cats bite most often and are traditionally served up almost every Friday night alongside our famous plates of Southern hushpuppies.

So how do you distinguish between the two? And how do you catch them?

Well, the blue cat is just that, a deeply colored slate-blue, grayish fish with a white underbelly. The channel cat also has a slate-blue coloration, only lighter, and except in the larger animals is always marked with irregular dark blotches down both sides of its body. If you want to set out on your own after either of these species, keep in mind they usually occupy large rivers, silted bayous, freshwater marshes, drainage canals, and land-locked impoundments.

Just about all catfish, even the little bullheads and mad-toms, could legitimately qualify as game fish on rod and reel because they put up a respectable battle when hooked relative to their size. This is especially true of blues and channels. The old-timers say that while you can catch catfish during the day, they bite best at night, preferring night crawlers, catalpa worms, small minnows or panfish, crawfish, shrimp, chicken gizzards, or stink baits fished directly on the bottom or such that the bait is suspended just off the bottom.

Newton Dufrene, who at 87 years old still catches his daily share of catfish on a trotline at a number of secret spots in the Pearl River Basin that he won't share with anybody, swears that nothing works as good as a square of Ivory soap.

"I'm here to tell you them big-jaw cats can smell that Ivory slickin' up and drifting downriver for miles," he proclaims as gospel. "Makes their mouths run water, it does! So they swim upstream along the slick line till they nosebump the soap and *whoop*—down the gullet it goes, hook and all. I got a friend who can catch 'em like that on juglines! But you gotta use Ivory soap. Catfish love Ivory soap! That's 'cuz it floats up off the bottom and they can find it easy."

THE SALTWATER SPECIES

Louisiana has two saltwater catfish species. One is consid-ered to be a worthy game fish, as well as great table fare (espe-cially for anyone wanting to whip up a batch of Cajun courtbouillon). Referred to most commonly as simply a "gafftop" or "sailcat," this scaleless marine creature, officially dubbed *gafftopsail catfish,* can be found in every part of the Louisiana coastal estuary as well as in the Gulf of Mexico.

While most fishermen don't actively seek out gafftops, they really don't complain all that much when they happen to catch one (even though the fish exudes a copious amount of mucosal slime during the battle that gets all over the monofilament). See, veteran saltwater anglers know that, filleted like a trout, a gafftop is tasty when rolled in cornmeal and deep-fried to a crunchy crispiness. They also know it broils well with lemon butter, poaches to perfection in soy-sauce stock, and comes out just right when barbecued on an open grill. But . . .

The gafftop's cousin, the seacat, better known as the *"hard-head,"* is generally accepted to be the pestilence of the coast! It would be safe to say that no fish God ever created is held in such disdain by man as the hardhead catfish.

The creature is never eaten because depending upon what *it* eats—*and remember, it's a scavenger that will try to ingest anything that was once organic*—it could either taste good or horribly bad! Obviously, nobody wants to experiment, so the fish is always roughed up, called a few choice names, and forcefully returned to the water.

But then, the hardhead doesn't know how to leave well enough alone either. To add insult to injury, not only will he pester every fisherman he'll ever come across, but before all is said and done he'll do his level best to try and bury one of his three venomous spines (one on the dorsal and two on the pectoral) into the fisherman's hand. Maybe it's true that when no one likes you, you get nasty!

Both the gafftop and hardhead (which some scientists believe possess a type of sonar) can be caught on a single- or double-drop rig using cut fish (mainly mullet), market shrimp, squid, and baby crabs. Actually, they'd probably take a chunk of bologna or a Vienna sausage if it were presented to them. Of course, the question is why would you ever want to feed a hardhead?

Now there is no way to wrap up this chapter without making

one final point, which may or may not be a revelation. Make no mistake about it, catfish featured at most seafood markets today versus those you go out and catch yourself are as different as ice cream and icebergs. Today's market catfish are almost always pond-raised catfish. They are clean and sweet and completely devoid of any fishy taste whatsoever because of their corn-fed diet.

So maybe these cats are not the musical. But from this point on, whether you buy 'em or fish 'em, at least you know the score! And that's the name of that tune.

CHAPTER 29

Trolling for Trout . . . Big Trout

Maybe elsewhere in the country—maybe even elsewhere in Louisiana—there are those who would put away their saltwater tackle during the dead of winter. But not in Southeast Louisiana! Not in Lake Borgne! And not at Shell Beach! Because in the dead of winter at Shell Beach, that's when you go "Trolling for Trout . . . Big Trout."

All these years I had trolled in only two places—offshore in the Gulf of Mexico and inshore in Lake Pontchartrain along the trestle. And at each of those spots, trolling is handled completely differently.

In the lake, for example, you start up the outboard, put it in gear, idle it as slow as it will go, begin playing out the lures on two or more baitcasting rods and reels loaded with leadcore line and tipped with Rat-L-Traps or QB-15 Bingos or some other legendary lures, and "troll" the baits behind the boat until a trout strikes (or until you get hung up on a piling and pop off the whole rig!).

Offshore, on the other hand, you rig up two or more rod-and-reel combinations, prop them down into the rod holders, bait up with "big stuff" like Coon-Pops or Konas or Drones, stagger the baits from tens to hundreds of feet behind the boat in the wheelwash (or off the outriggers), and "troll" at about 1,100 RPM until a tuna or wahoo or bonito or marlin strikes.

Yet would you believe that in all their years, that's not the way Kenny Campo and Pete Agnelly ever trolled? Not at Shell Beach, anyway! And Kenny and Pete have the enviable reputation of catching some of the biggest trout ever taken on a hook. In the dead of winter. By trolling. Shell Beach style!

"People use a variety of plugs when they troll for winter trout down here," Campo explained to me as we eased into one of the many bayous that drain the Shell Beach-Ycloskey-Hopedale marsh into Lake Borgne. "Some use soft-plastic Cocahoe tails, for instance. Some use hard-plastic diving baits. And others try the weedless metal spoons. But my family—as well as most of my friends—have been doing this kind of fishing for a long time, and as far as we're concerned nothing beats the queen-size chartreuse split-tail beetle with the hotspot, threaded onto a half-ounce plain leadhead jig. That's a killer combination, pod'nuh!"

Speaking of friends, one of Kenny's closest, Pete Agnelly, couldn't wait to chime into this conversation. "Yeah, but it's not just tie on a lure and pull it behind the boat, Frank. There are some rules you gotta follow! For example, you want to use only enough weight to get the bait barely bouncing off the bottom. If you're too light on the lead and the bait rides too high in the water column, you'll never get a strike. By the same token, if you're too heavy on the lead and the jig head digs into the grass and muck and mud, you won't get a strike there either."

"So how do you know when you got it right?" I asked Pete. Before he could respond, Campo answered!

"First you play out the line about 30, 40, or 50 yards behind the boat. Then, depending upon how fast you're trolling, you increase or decrease the weight of the jig head until you can barely detect a slight bumping sensation as the lure is pulled along."

"Yeah, if you can't feel the bottom, you're not down where the big trout are," Agnelly added. "And if, on the other hand, you feel a lot of snagging going on, like the hook is grabbing everything on the bottom and nearly ripping the rod out of your hand, then you're way too deep!"

But let's back up here for a minute. You obviously get the picture of what's going on in this type of trolling, right? You have one, two, or three fishermen aboard the boat. Each one is fishing one rod and reel (not several of them stuck up in the rod holders as they do on Lake Pontchartrain and offshore).

"Another thing—your boat is being pulled ahead by the bow trolling motor," Agnelly stressed, "not being pushed by the big stern-mounted Mercury, or Evinrude, or Johnson, or Yamaha."

"Right—you're trolling with the trolling motor," Campo reemphasized, "and you need to move at, say, a good walking speed. Of course, you gotta regulate that with the throttle, and that's going to depend upon how strong or how weak the tide is, how brisk the wind is blowing, or how shallow or how deep the water is. But once you get it right, you won't believe the size of the trout you can catch!"

The entire premise is based on the biological fact that in the dead of winter, big trout (calculate the average to be in the five pounds apiece neighborhood) tend to hole up in some of the deepest bayous and centerline channels. The rationale is simple: deeper water will be warmer in winter than water found on shallow reefs and flats. So consequently, if you can suspend an artificial lure just off the bottom of a warm-water channel and twitch it erratically (popping the rod tip periodically), then you should keep an accurate count of how many fish you put in the boat, because it won't take you long to get a full limit.

"Yeah, but folks need to know that they're not gonna catch fish as fast by trolling in winter as they'd catch them by cast and retrieve in the midst of a big school in summer," Campo interjected. "The action is definitely slower; but, good God, when you do catch 'em they're monsters!"

Agnelly stopped fishing for a few minutes to show me how to rig the terminal tackle for wintertime trolling. "Frank, you can do it one of two ways. You can either fish a straight jig head and beetle off the mainline monofilament, or you can do what me and Kenny like to do best—rig a monofilament loop shock leader about 18 inches long, attached to the mainline by a snap swivel, and ending with the queen-size chartreuse beetle threaded onto a half-ounce jig head."

So where does all this wintertime trout catching go on? The two veteran masters will tell you that there must be over 50 bayous and canals between Shell Beach and Hopedale where trolling is nothing short of phenomenal. But both Campo and Agnelly readily admit that they tend to favor Bayou Hasousse, Bayou St. Malo, Bayou Pedro, Bayou Grande, Kenny's Bayou, and many of the deepwater cuts on the famed Louisiana Marsh.

"What you need to do," Campo confides, "is try to find a bayou where the tide is moving good, where the water is nice and clean, where the bottom varies along its length from continuous flatline to interspersed deep holes, and where there is some obvious baitfish activity present.

"Then you troll a significant stretch of the bayou—say, 100 yards or so—varying the speed. If you come upon a productive spot, you'll no doubt catch a trout—maybe catch a half-dozen trout! And when you catch those trout, be sure you turn around and pull past those prime spots again and again and again. Maybe not the entire length of the bayou will produce fish. Maybe only a small portion will. But then that's all you need!"

Campo and Agnelly also agree that not every bayou, not every twist and turn, and not every drop-off will yield success. But they will also tell you that there is only one way to determine just how good a fishing spot really is.

"You bundle up, you get out there, and you try every single one of them!" Agnelly laughs. "Then when you zero in on the right ones, you don't tell a soul—I mean not anybody!"

The two looked at each other and grinned connivingly.

"Well, okay, I mean you could tell us!"

CHAPTER 30

Head 'Em Off at the Pass

Some of the biggest bull reds caught along the Louisiana coastline consistently come from the barrier island passes 12 miles below Cocodrie. Here's why they're there and how to catch them!

The 5 A.M. alarm fractured the silence of the bunkhouse at Coco Marina, and myself and 12 of my most zealous fishing-school students, gratuitously dubbed "The Lucky Thirteen," rolled out from between the sheets. The obvious was immediate—we didn't have to switch on the weather channel to get the picture. The entire building we rested so comfortably and obliviously in all night long was now rhythmically vibrating, steadfastly resisting the nudging of the southeasterly winds.

"Oh, it's gonna be fun crossing Terrebonne Bay this morning!" one of the pack mumbled to his bunkmates.

"I don't know why they always hoist the hurricane flags whenever I get a chance to go fishing!" his buddy responded.

"Anybody bring along the TripTone?"

"Aw, you don't need none of that!" came a shout from the bathroom over the hum of an electric razor. "I always stash a jar of pickled pig's feet in my ditty bag—a couple of those bad boys for breakfast and the swells won't bother you at all!"

With all the exuberance of a troupe of stand-up comedians, my team kept the one-liners coming; but it was all just part of the drill designed to get the morning off to a good start. There was nary a man—nor boy—in the condo ready to change the original plan. At supper the night before, I had told the crew what marina owner Johnny Glover, and his charter captains Pecky Bourg, Eugene Foret, and Aaron Robichaux, had promised . . . big, *big* bull reds in the surf at Little Pass. And this morning it was time for our plan to be put into action.

About an hour after the last quip, two boats had settled side by side on anchor, riding the four-foot swells over the centerline channel of Little Pass on the western edge of East Timbalier Island. The cracked-crab baits tossed off the stern weren't even wet good before the lines went down and the shouts went up.

"There he is! That's the first one!" Captain Eugene proclaimed to my crew as we all glanced portside at Captain Aaron's boat, cresting beside us. "See the bend in that rod? That's what big bull reds do to them!" By the time he finished the sentence, four other rods had assumed the same arch.

Traditionally, every January through March, the outer barrier islands in Terrebonne Bay become home base for some of the biggest bull redfish that swim along coastal Louisiana. They haunt the beaches and sand flats, cruising the pounding whitewater surf for tidbits to quell their insatiable appetites. But the heaviest of the heavyweights lurk in the tidal passes.

Off to port, I could see Pecky and Aaron dipping, scooping, and hoisting redfish into Aaron's boat, *The Shaka.* The two captains moved in unison, almost as if choreographed in an aquatic ballet, just in an attempt to keep up with the fishing talents of their crew on board.

Back aboard Eugene's boat, *The Bushwhacker,* I was straining to tame my third fish of the morning. As I tugged, and pumped, and took up line, I remembered what I had read once in A. J. McClane's *Fishing Encyclopedia* about these bronze-back monsters—that they range anywhere from 25 to 45 pounds apiece, that they feed incessantly on crabs, snails, minnows, mullets, and almost anything else that appears edible, and that for the most part the so-called big bulls usually turn out to be big "sows."

"Cracked crab is the way to catch 'em, Frank," Captain Eugene leaned over to tell me, interrupting my thoughts.

"Without a doubt they prefer crabs over everything else in their diet. I honestly believe that they'd try to cross a busy interstate highway at drive-time just to get to a hunk of crab. And that's how we fish them most of the time here at Cocodrie."

At this point in the trip, my students had quickly gotten the hang of rigging, baiting, casting, hooking, and fighting the quarry we had set out after. So I whispered to Captain Eugene that since this was a "field trip" for them, designed to put into practice what they'd been taught in the classroom, we ought to leave them to their studies. Besides, it gave Eugene time to pick fish up off the boat floor and tally up the limit; and it gave me time to break for a soft drink and recall some of the many conversations Johnny Glover and I had had about red-fish over the years in the restaurant at Coco Marina.

"Frank, bull reds along the Louisiana coast are rather unique animals," I remember him saying, as we dipped toasted garlic bread into the Wine Island Shrimp sauce. "Sure, they range the full length of the Atlantic and Gulf coasts of the United States, say from about Massachusetts all the way over to Texas. But in Louisiana, they're not as seasonal a species, which means they don't do a whole lot of migration.

"Most of the year they stay offshore here. But from November through May, when it's time for them to spawn, they come into our bays, they roam up and down our sand beaches, and they skirt back and forth from the gulfside to the marshside through any of a number of breaks in the barrier islands—Wine Island Pass, Whiskey Pass, Little Pass, and so forth.

"And that's the best time to catch 'em as far as I'm concerned because it's when we can target in on the real jammers of the bunch—the bigger bulls."

The firing of both Yamahas put an abrupt end to my recollections. "Frank, we kinda drifted off the channel shelf," Captain Eugene shouted over the drone of the engines, dropping the outboards in gear, "so I'm going to pull us up about 25 yards and reposition the boat."

I nodded in approval and held onto the wheel for him as

he hoisted the anchor. When he returned to the helm, he began to explain to me and my students the rationale for the move.

"These fish like to browse with the current that funnels through the passes," he said. "So you have to set yourself up to be able to cast smack dab in the middle of that current. See, what happens is the moving water pulls bait—crabs, mullets, Cocahoe minnows—along with it, and the tide tumbles it out of control through the channel. This gives the big reds an ambush advantage. I mean, those little fish and crabs are frantically trying to swim through the current, and the last thing they notice are those big open mouths waiting to turn them into dinner! It's just that simple."

"But how do you know when you're in a spot that's holding fish, Gene?" I asked, watching him reset the anchor.

"Fish slicks!" he shouted back to me from the bow. "It's a surefire way to find 'em every time." He reached over the console and turned off the ignition. "Okay, guys, go get 'em," he continued. "See, Frank, when these fish are actively feeding, they crunch up what they're feeding on in their powerful jaws. So the natural oils in all those minnows and crabs and mullets come rising to the top—kinda like an oil slick, which is what it really is, only it's fish oil. There are a couple of them behind the boat right now!"

Needless to say, for the rest of the morning my crew pointed out every one that popped up, in between catching and releasing fish, of course (they had had their limits in the box long ago).

If bull reds are grubbing anywhere in the area, you should have one or more on the lines in 15 minutes or less. If you've gotten no hookups within that allotted time period, either change locations in the pass or move to another pass. Usually, the former is sufficient.

Veterans who regularly pursue the bulls will quickly let you know that you need the right kind of tackle to catch these monsters, tackle that includes a seven-foot heavy-action graphite rod, fitted with a stout saltwater reel—like an Ambassaseur 6500-C3 or Shimano Triton 100. The best terminal rigging consists of a 4/0 Kahle hook, tied onto a 40-pound shock leader about 14 inches long, and connected by a barrel swivel to the monofilament coming off your reel. A two-ounce egg sinker will get the rigging to the bottom. All that's left is to take a blue crab, remove the top shell, break it into halves, and run the hook through the main swimmeret on one of the halves.

All of Johnny Glover's guides suggest you use 20- or 25-pound-test, "big-game-grade" monofilament for these giants.

"Personally I wouldn't go any heavier than 30-pound test," Johnny pointed out. "You sacrifice too much casting distance and line sensitivity. And keep in mind that in rough white water along the beaches, or in high-current pass channels, you need that sensitivity to feel the 'bite.'"

Actually, what you feel is more like a "thump" at the end of your line. What happens is the bull red picks up the crab from the bottom, crushes it in its mouth, then swallows it. So to catch them time and again, you must avoid the tendency to set the hook the moment you feel the bite (this is okay if you're fishing rat reds with artificials or spoons or even live Cocahoe minnows—but not for bull reds on cracked crab).

"I find it's best if, when you feel the *thump,* you wait until the line tightens up and all the slack is gone," Captain Aaron explained. "Then, and only then, do you lean forward as far as you can and rear back. You got to give them time to eat it. If it's a big bull red you've stuck, he'll make the first power run; and the moment the run starts, reset the hook at least two more times in quick short jerks. It'll bury the barb and provide less of a chance for the fish to throw or 'spit' the hook."

Here are a few more suggested tactics:

1. Be sure you have your reel drag set properly. These fish unleash brute strength during their famed "power runs." If the star drag is winched too tightly, the head shake synonymous with a bull red on the line and the fish's sudden surges will snap the most premium monofilament.

2. Never "horse" a big bull. When he wants to run, let him

run. A little patience on your part is all that's needed. Enjoy the battle. If you've done everything right, you're the odds-on winner anyway.

3. And unless you want a onetime wall mount, I heartily suggest you catch and release all the big reds you bring to the boat. Contrary to what you might have heard, they're really not all that great as table fare. Small reds—the 10-pound-and-under fish we refer to as "rat reds"—are flaky, tender, and delicious, a treat on any connoisseur's table. The old bulls, however, have a coarse, stringy, sinewy texture. But more importantly, the old bulls are the breeders—they're the ones who will produce the next year's crop for years to come. Put 'em back!

Anyway, to get back to how I started this chapter, every one of my students ended up catching a limit of reds and returning to the water at least three times that much (to say nothing of all the bull drums we got into). And despite the four-foot swells and the greasy egg and sausage sandwiches, only two of them got seasick (mainly because the guy with the TripTone came up with a short supply).

But back at the marina everyone agreed that the happiest of "The Lucky Thirteen" were two little boys—Jimmy and Sean—who had never caught fish so big in their lives and who these days attach a whole new meaning to the phrase . . . *head 'em off at the pass!*

CHAPTER 31

From Back-a Golden Meadow

Dozens of lakes renowned for holding schools of trout . . . winding bayous that afford the perfect habitat for cruising red-fish . . . shallow-water flats where doormat flounders stack up like cordwood . . . deep centerline channels where black drums lurk . . . outcroppings of natural oyster reefs that serve as chow-lines for shell-crunching packs of sheepshead . . . and open access to the remaining barrier islands for calm-day fishing of the open waters of the Gulf of Mexico. You can get to all of these spots "From Back-a Golden Meadow"!

It never changes! Every morning of his life, when he sits down to his regular 5 A.M. breakfast at Rose's Cafe, at least one fisherman—local or chartered client—will ask him the question.

"So where did you find 'em yesterday, John? In the hole back there by the spot? Along the reef where Vernon and Larry were Tuesday? In Catfish Lake at the pilings? Out by the new cut that opened at East Timbalier?"

For John ("Hawkeye") Aucoin, this is all just shop talk. He and his fellow guides share in it every morning between breakfast mouthfuls of Spanish omelets, or toast-sopping twos over easy, or low-fat short stacks with molasses and several shots of strong bayou-style coffee.

But to this select Cajun cadre of guides, who daily ply the waters between Cut Off and Grand Isle from access points having such names as Chick's and Besson's in search of creel limits for their clients, such impromptu conversation is considered *coded tongue* that only they understand. Their references are to the literally hundreds of spots Aucoin and his colleagues have found to fish over the years, to more they need to share, and to even more they need to find and keep up with. But each of these professional fishermen, and especially Aucoin, admits to being fortunate that God has given him a *turf* that by all accounts is nothing less than outstanding, where day in and day out he can do in life what he wants to do and take novice sportsmen to catch fish without ever having to go any farther than *back-a Golden Meadow*.

"Frank, there is no better place to fish in all of Louisiana," Aucoin told me confidently one evening before a memorable fishing trip, downing his last bite of pork roti at a roadside restaurant in Cut Off. He pushed his plate away, wiped his mouth, and folded his arms in front of him, settling in for what he anticipated was going to be several hours of talking about his favorite place on earth. So I sat back and let him talk.

"The good Lord built an estuary here," he began, "and He filled it with everything it needed to hold fish—oysters, shrimp, crabs, and snails. Then inside this big space He gave us fresh water, salt water, and brackish water, just so we wouldn't get bored with just one flavor. And if that weren't enough, 45 minutes by boat and you're out on the open waters of the Gulf of Mexico!"

Every time Aucoin opens his mouth, he speaks from experience dating back to when he was six years old. Although professionally guiding only since 1991, he was born and raised (as they say) "down on the bayou" and fished virtually every cut, every outfall, every trainaisse, every slough, and every pipeline canal since he was tall enough to lean on a pushpole and get the pirogue to move.

"You got to look at *back-a Golden Meadow* like it was the hub of a big wheel," he continued. "Take the spoke to the north and you head up to the Bully Camp on the Pointe au Chien Wildlife Management Area. Take the south spoke and you drop down to Leeville, the Fourchon, on out to the islands.

The spoke to the west puts you outside of Cocodrie. And an eastward direction out of Leeville, say, situates you at Grand Isle and Caminada. Of course, the most important part of all of this is that these are real fish-catching spots, and *highly productive* fish-catching spots at that!"

The former marine electrician and refrigeration mechanic is adamant, though, that to consistently catch fish *back-a Golden Meadow*, you have to be willing to do some dry-land studying.

"Let me see if I can play the professor here for a minute and give you about 20 years worth of details that you can pick and choose from as basic background. Then you take off from there.

"First, keep in mind that from Cut Off to the gulf is a whole lot of territory; so without being selective and discriminating you just aren't going to stop anywhere and fill an ice chest to the brim. I also recommend that any fisherman—veteran or greenhorn—wanting to come here to fish first learn a few basics. You want to remember things like:

"1. In all of Louisiana, we have the greatest protection from both east and west wind right here *back-a Golden Meadow.* There's always protected water here, so even on those horribly windy days we can find a good place to fish, and *catch* fish while we're working at it!

"2. Learning to fish *back-a Golden Meadow* takes a little bit of familiarity. You might first want to fish with me or one of the other guides just to learn something about the lay of the land. It's not hard to find your way around, but you have to invest a little time in it.

"3. Learn early on that *back-a Golden Meadow* is good fishing year round, but it requires different techniques at different times of the year. Summertime tactics, for example, are cut and dried and by the book. Wintertime tactics are purely instinctive. Here's what I mean—in spring and summer, go ahead and fish the open lakes from Raccourci to Timbalier; in the fall, though, backtrack northward to Deep Lake, Felicity, Gray Duck, and Catfish. In spring and summer, fish fast with surface topwaters or smoke-colored grubs. In the fall, slow the baits down. In the dead of winter, fish deep and fish dead slow."

At this stage of the interview, Aucoin repeatedly tapped his finger on the table to reemphasize a point. "Frank, generally, though, even a novice fisherman can come *back-a Golden Meadow* and catch fish if he fishes the main channels, the main lakes, the dead-end canals, the sulfur mine, Catfish Lake, Bay Savin, Little Gray Duck Lake, Big Gray Duck Lake, Lake Raccourci, Bayou Blue, Lake Felicity, Deep Lake, Old Lady Lake, and Timbalier Bay. And you can reach every one of these spots from Golden Meadow within 30 minutes. Ain't a whole lot of other fishing haunts in Louisiana can make that offer!"

Aucoin began his guiding career in 1991 as a sideline weekend activity. But all that has long since changed. Today, after wearing out four state-of-the-art boats, each one bigger and more sophisticated than the last, he runs over 200 U.S. Coast Guard-licensed charter trips every year.

"I tell rookies and first-timers who come to fish *back-a Golden Meadow* to start off in the pipelines, fish the oyster reefs, concentrate on the old weirs, never pass up a broken island, and especially look for shallow areas. But with every revolution of the propeller, you gotta think caution!

"*Back-a Golden Meadow* is a unique spot and provides outstanding fishing for virtually anyone—you can fish a 12-foot boat here as well as you can fish a 24-footer. But first, you got to know what you're chasing and you got to know exactly where you're chasing it.

"Go slow if you don't know where you are! Remember you're not in a hurry. We've had fish down here for thousands of years—they'll be here for a while longer. You go roaring over what looks like a deep lake and you could come up on a reef that'll tear the entire lower unit off your outboard!"

At this point, I was beginning to question my decision not to do this interview on a tape recorder. John now had me scribbling notes at the same speed that he was talking. Clearly he was into his soul now—it was disclosure time.

"Use your charts. Use your color maps. Take them on the boat with you. Don't leave them home. At a place as big as *back-a Golden Meadow*, you're going to need them. Best artificial baits for *back-a Golden Meadow* include the plain smoke grub and the smoke with glitter beetle or Cocahoe tail, the emerald-green beetle with the black tail, and the cream-colored grub. Of course, I got to tell you that I honestly in my heart and soul believe that the best bait is the one bait you're most confident in.

"I also believe that you should always bring along live Cocahoes. It's the one way to ensure that you'll catch fish and bypass a wasted day if, for whatever the reason, you can't get them—no matter what the species—to take artificials."

I had been scrawling notes so rapidly and so obliviously, I hadn't realized that our waitress had long ago cleared the table and up to now Aucoin had had her pour him about a half-dozen coffee refills. Looking around and seeing her nowhere in sight, he whispered to me, "If we're going to wrap up this story tonight, I got to have one more shot."

He headed off across the restaurant to find the coffeepot, so I flipped the page in my notebook and took the opportunity to jot down some personal observations. John and I have fished together regularly for years, so the notes I scrunched between the lines I had often heard quoted as chapter and verse out on the open marsh.

Have patience. Relax. Be quiet. Start fishing way away from the fish you're chasing, and then ease into them slowly without a whole lot of noise and confusion. See that trolling motor? Next to your rod and reel it is the most important piece of equipment on the boat—when the fish won't come to you, it brings you to the fish. Oh, and carry a pushpole too. There are times when it's just what you need to work your way into an area where the fish are holed up!

"Let's go," he coaxed, returning to the table, tugging my pen out of my hand in midsentence inscription, and shoving it down into my shirt pocket. "We done ate all of the food and drank all the coffee. We got to go home b'fore they make some more! Not only that, you got to get some sleep—I want you to meet me for breakfast at 4:30 at Rose's. I want to be sitting on top this spot I know about a half-hour before the fish even wake up!"

Out in the parking lot, as he climbed into his Suburban with Hawkeye Fishing Team and his sponsors' logos painted all over the windows, he shouted back at me, "You don't have to write this down, but if you're planning on ending the story by asking me if I'd ever think of fishing someplace else, the answer is *no, 'cuz there ain't no better place to fish than back-a Golden Meadow!"*

He let out a Cajun-accented high-pitched laugh, slammed the door, and drove off into the night. And as I watched the lights from the businesses along the highway shimmer on the ripples in Bayou Lafourche, I thought to myself, you know he could very well be right!

CHAPTER 32

All I Want for Christmas Is . . .

So do you leave your Yuletide wishes entirely up to the whim of your spouse? Or is the best method to shop on the recommendation of those outdoor experts who regularly send you that mail-order catalogue? Or maybe you should just ask for gift money so that you can go down to the local sporting-goods store and pick out your own present so that you get the right thing in the first place! Or what about taking the traditional route and writing out a note to Jolly Ol' St. Nick that says, "All I Want for Christmas Is . . . "?

So here you got this big fat bearded dude who has never worn anything but a baggy old red suit,

. . . never rode in anything but an antiquated sleigh, let alone a pirogue or an ATV,

. . . never been outside of the Arctic Circle except after dark for like maybe two days a year,

. . . knows so little about fishing—any kind of fishing—he couldn't distinguish between a char and a chinquapin,

. . . can't even make mention of, let alone advise you on, the sport of deer hunting for fear of the catastrophic impact it would have on eight specialized members of his transportation team and the other one with the shiny red nose,

. . . and *this* is the guy you're gonna write a letter to, giving him carte blanche to pick out, at his own discretion, using his own judgment, your Christmas rod and reel and tackle box and boat and motor and trailer and GPS and char-grill and shotgun and deck shoes!

Wait a minute! Wait a minute!! What say we rethink this Christmas gift thing?

A very good friend of mine—an old-timer, in fact—once told me, "Pickin' out hunting and fishing stuff, Frank, is like pickin' out a wife! Even though there's a whole lot out there to pick from, still and all you want to pick your own!" So why should things be any different at Christmas?

Over the years I've fished all year long with fellow sportsmen who used tackle their well-meaning wives bought them at Christmas. That's a sad sight, y'all. No one should have to witness that!

Over the years I've hunted with fellow members down at the duck camp who have attempted to bring home the makings of an occasional duck stew using the gun the better half bought on sale from the teenage shooting expert working behind the Christmas counter at WallyWorld! That's even sadder yet!

So having duly noted such dilemmas, here is how I suggest you go about procuring the correct outdoor-oriented gifts from wives, lovers, children, relatives, neighbors, business associates, and everyone else you suspect will be presenting you the spirit of the season in material form.

1. Contract with a local computer guru good at cable-box tampering to have the brand-name outdoor equipment you want for Christmas subliminally infused into soap operas and cartoons (and, yes, even MTV, should you be the parent of a teenage gift-giver) for your wife and children to see.

2. Leave catalogues, brochures, and flyers from your preferred sporting-goods purveyors lying open around the house—especially in such inconspicuous places as under the TV controller, beside the makeup mirror, next to the checkbook, on top of the ice-cream bars in the freezer, or on the magazine stool adjacent to the toilet.

3. Leave those catalogues open to the pages to which you want attention directed. If you believe that, in your family, subtlety won't work, you might want to highlight the selected gifts unobtrusively, perhaps by underlining them with an international-orange Dayglo pen, or double circling them

with a wide-tip red Marks-A-Lot, or even splash-blotting them with Just for Men, which you reserve for the purpose after touching up your beard and sideburns.

4. But if none of the above achieves the desired effect, then take the campaign a bit farther by clipping the actual color pictures of the things you want out of catalogues or ads and placing them where they will be noticed—in the wife's underwear drawer, for example, or on the chip clip that holds the top of the Oreo bag closed, or Scotch taped to the sheets of toilet paper so that they'll be viewed in kaleidoscopic form as they come off the roll.

5. Finally, if none of the methods heretofore mentioned works, then perhaps scribbling out a categorical listing of the things you really and truly want for Christmas in blazing red lipstick across the bathroom mirror might well be in order!

Thus far, this entire chapter has been penned exclusively for the gift *recipient.* But what about suggestions of appropriate items—generic items—to give the gift *giver?* Here's what your ol' buddy Kris Kringle Frank recommends:

1. The all-purpose multitool! You've seen 'em—almost everybody makes 'em. They have like 76 tools all in one! Makes no difference whether the person you give this to is a hunter or a fisherman, this is a piece of equipment he'll strap on his belt and use (or at least display as male-macho plumage).

2. A Shimano Calcutta reel! Yeah, I know he's probably got a jillion reels, but why not give him the ultimate best there is? I can tell you it's hard for Santa to part with these; but if you elect to go the retail route I'd just pick out a charge card he has with a high credit limit and sign it off!

3. A portable spooling station or line winder. That's one of those gizmos that sits on your workbench and you put a spool of monofilament line on it and it fills your reel without twisting and stretching the line. This is one of those gifts you always wanted, but you just don't buy it for yourself—someone else has to buy it for you! And then you're really happy, whether you ever use it or not.

4. A cast net! See, there's a good chance he's telling all his friends that he's not catching a whole lot of fish because he just isn't an artificial-bait fisherman. So get him a cast net, suggest he take it on every trip from now on to pick up live bait, and then see what excuse he comes up with!

5. How about an Edgemaker Pro Sharpening Hone? Good for both hunters and fishermen, it gets skinning and filleting knives razor sharp! Kinda cheap, sure, but you don't have to give it a lot of thought.

6. A handheld CB or VHF radio makes a great gift for both hunters and fishermen ('cuz you can get just as lost on the water as you can in the woods). So while the recipient sportsman is out there screaming his lungs out for help, if you were thoughtful enough to have given him a gift of state-of-the-art communications equipment, even one of the newest cell phones, maybe someone will be able to hear his screams.

Of course, you got your usual boat covers, battery chargers, hunting jackets, rain suits, deck shoes, earmuffs, drink holders, weather radios, pointy-nose pliers, catfish flippers, electric filleting knives, emergency tool sets, art-deco shell buckets—the list goes on and on. I don't know, though. Folks have always told me that for any of these suggestions to take on any meaning, one must already be caught up in the magic of Christmas.

Maybe when all is said and done, going along with the big fat guy in the red suit isn't such a bad idea after all! In fact, now that I've actually written all this stuff out for you and had time to read and reread it while I was editing it, may I—*in the true spirit of the season*—suggest that you get out a piece of paper, then take a pen, and just below the top left margin write, *"Dear Santa, all I want for Christmas is . . . !"*

CHAPTER 33

Fishin' by the Numbers—Gospel 1

HOW TO FISH SPECKLED TROUT

It goes without saying that most of us veteran anglers take the entire process of wetting a line and catching a fish for granted. We assume, erroneously of course, that all the high-tech fish-finding and baitcasting we've been doing all these years are like second nature and automatically understood by every other fisherman. But oftentimes—in fact, more often than not—the neophyte has no idea what we're doing nor why!

This has always been the reason why our brothers-in-law, next-door neighbors, business associates, fellow workers, lodge buddies, the guy sitting next to us in the barbershop, and the deacon praying behind us in the pew at Sunday mass continue to ask whoever will listen the most basic of fishing questions:

"So, what's a Carolina rig?"

"What's it mean to 'fish a falling tide'?"

"How do you hook a live shrimp?"

"What's a Kahle hook, anyway?"

"Is it worthwhile to fish in the wintertime?"

Those and dozens of other rudimentary questions appear to be endless.

As a professional writer and disseminator of outdoor information, I am forever amazed by the inquiries I get day in and day out at my answering service, over my 1-800 number, on my e-mail, and in the notes jotted on scraps of sandwich bags and stashed into crumpled-up envelopes that arrive at my desk daily via the post office. No one ever wants to know the ichthyological makeup of the dorsal-ray configuration of a deepwater whiting. Instead, they just want to know what color the popping cork should be on a redfish rig! Really basic stuff. Because they honestly don't know!

Well, may I humbly beg forgiveness of everyone who ever picked up and read anything I've written concerning fishing over the past 40-something years. I truly apologize for being so vague (or rather, so presumptuous!). I promise each of you that through the chapter and verse of this book, you'll become acutely acquainted with "Fishin' 101—The Commandments." Oh, I'm sure that the obvious oversimplification will bore some of you to tears; but then again, maybe it will be a subtle refresher course.

So, starting with speckled trout, here's how you fish 'em . . . *by the numbers:*

1. Connect the boat, motor, and trailer to the pickup. If you don't have a boat, you're going to have a tough time fishing at most of the popular bankfishing spots. Most of them will be either crowded with other fishermen, totally overfished, or in some stage of conversion from a bankfishing spot to a garbage dump. If you want to be guaranteed a somewhat successful trip and you don't have a boat, rent one or go with someone who does.

2. Choose a launch site where you have good access to productive fishing grounds. If you don't know where these places are, ask local anglers, or call TV and/or radio personalities who do fishing shows and engage in a bit of conversation with them (making mental notes you can use). You should also read just about anything you can get your hands on concerning fishing for trout in the areas you intend to fish. You also want to watch those TV shows and listen to those radio programs that deal with trout fishing in your intended spots. And finally, spend a lot of time at the boat launches talking to veteran fishermen—they might not always give you their secret spots, but if they sense you're genuinely interested they'll generously share their tips and tricks with you.

3. But back to the launch for a moment. Before you back down the ramp, make sure the plug is in the transom, remove the tie-down straps, disconnect the winch hook from the boat at the front of the trailer, and have the castaway rope available for the person who will hold onto the boat as you launch it. This is also the time to check and see that lifejackets, extra rope, a paddle, an anchor, and perhaps a couple of mud poles are in the boat.

4. When you're in the water, start and idle the engine to warm it up before heading out across the marsh (oh—you'll first need to prime the gas-line bulb).

5. If the plan is to fish on the inside (which is best in late fall and winter), familiar yourself with some of the popular hotspots you've been told about by referencing and intently studying the appropriate charts and maps as often as possible before you head out on open uncharted water. By the way, the "inside" is defined as any protected water—canals, bayous, ponds, lagoons, shallow bays, shoreline marsh. The opposite of "inside" is "open water, outside, or offshore."

6. When it comes to finding speckled trout on these waterways, there are several ways to do it. Look for telltale signs— you might see birds (mainly seagulls) feeding; you might notice a virtual armada of boats clustered in one area; you might see a "slick" pop up to the surface (this appears as a shiny spot that looks as if someone dropped oil overboard). And you can always go to those specific locations (points on the marsh, pockets along the shoreline, rigs at the ends of pipeline canals) you've been told about by fellow fishermen or articles or TV reports. Be sure to try fishing all these spots. But let's look at each of these scenarios individually.

If you notice birds diving, ease your boat into position so that you drift into the flocks with the wind against your back, casting as you go. Whatever you do, don't run into the flocks and break them up! Once they separate, you will no longer have any idea where the main trout school is.

See, the reason gulls dive is that trout (or some other

predatory fish) are in the process of feeding on shrimp and baitfish. Like fine-tuned rodeo cutting horses, the trout cordon off a segment of shrimp and separate them from the remainder of the raft. Then, as they feed on this encapsulated ball of shrimp, numerous individual shrimp are hurt or killed and float to the surface. The birds dive and feed on these injured or dying baitfish, precisely giving away the position of the speckled trout that lie directly under them!

And always fancast as you drift. Cast perpendicular to the boat, to the back of the boat, and to the front of the boat. It is essential that you find the area occupied by the fish (in other words, "the school"). Once you do and you get into them, ease the anchor over and fish the school hard! Usually, the appropriate bait for this particular scenario is a quarter-ounce jig head fitted with either a white, glow, or smoke-colored grub or split-tail beetle. You might also try a chartreuse Coca-hoe tail on a quarter-ounce jig head. And by the way, you don't have to buy an assortment of painted heads—*unpainted ones work just fine!*

While sometimes it's pitifully misleading, a cluster of boats usually means somebody in the armada is catching fish (which has attracted all the other fishermen to infringe upon the spot). These areas are definitely worth sampling because at times they do produce fantastic catches of trout. But just remember to exercise the utmost courtesy when approaching the cluster of boats. Unless you delicately "sneak" in, you could ruin the fishing for everyone. And don't crowd! Judge your presence by asking yourself if you'd want someone to do to you what you're fixin' to do to them. Works every time!

Like boat clusters, slicks can be awfully misleading, but as a good fisherman you just got to stop and try them. What's misleading about them is you have no idea what kind of fish caused the slick. It could be voraciously feeding trout or reds, or it could be a ball of rummaging hardhead catfish. That's because slicks form when fish (1) bite down on their food, releasing oils into the water, and (2) regurgitate portions of what they've just eaten during the feeding process. Regardless, however, you're almost compelled to stop and fish a slick! Oh, yeah—and like fishing the birds, kill the engine and drift into the slicks so that you don't disperse the school. Of course, if a slick produces no action within a few minutes, write it off and move on.

CHAPTER 34

Fishin' by the Numbers—Gospel 2

HOW TO FISH REDS AND DRUM AT THE POINTS AND IN THE POCKETS

What fish do you find clustered around marsh points? What is a marsh point? How can you recognize it? Which side of the point do you fish? What species occupies a pocket in the marsh? How do I know a pocket when I see one? Describe the difference between a pocket and an indentation in the shoreline. Where do you usually catch fish in a pipeline canal? Is a pipeline canal the same as a "dead-end" canal?

To begin at the beginning, a "marsh point" is a section of the grassy shoreline that protrudes out into the water—it could be pointy, hooked, flattened, or rounded, but it is still defined as a marsh *point*. Those speckled trout we discussed in the last gospel could hold on a marsh point, but more than likely they will be located a short distance off the point in deeper water where the shelf drops off.

This is because the baitfish on either side of the point are usually jostled about in the tide or current, causing them to swirl downward in the eddies into deeper water off the shelf. And that's where the trout wait for them in ambush. Of course, having said that, it's possible that any trout in the area might be as close to the shoreline as they can get.

Generally, though, redfish and drum (and, yes, flounder and stingrays) stake claim to the shallows on a point. Oftentimes you can actually see them "finning" (which means they're up against the grass so shallow that their fins actually protrude from the water). Reds and drum and flounder grub right up against the grassline, snacking continuously on small baitfish, tiny crabs, clams, and snails that cling to the grasses that grow from the water's edge.

These fish usually stay "down-flow" of the tide or current, so that it pushes baitfish in their direction, thereby making for an easy meal. To put it another way, points are *ambush* spots where redfish or flounder, for example, can hide on one side of the point and patiently wait to surprise a small fish or crab coming around the other side—*the blind side!*—of the point.

So where do you fish the point? Your first cast should be made as close to the shoreline as you can get on the "down-flow side" of the point. Go first for the fish already in hiding! And assume that the fish, whether it be a red, drum, or flounder, will be facing the grass, waiting for something tasty to crawl out of the grass and into the water.

What does this tell you to do as an angler? It tells you to cast so close to the grass you put bruise marks on it! You need to get the bait ahead of the fish, not behind it. A cast ahead of it will get the fish's attention; a cast behind it will undoubtedly spook him and cause him to race away.

Techniques are essentially similar in the pockets (a pocket is a deep, hollowed-out indentation in the marsh grassline), with the only difference being that it is principally redfish you'll be after in the pockets. What you do is slowly—and very quietly—drift up to the opening of the pocket, placing yourself right in the middle of the opening so that you can cast and cover both hemi-arcs (left and right). Then ease the anchor down (or better yet, stick a marsh pole in the bottom and tie off the boat—this makes a lot less noise than an anchor). Now make long casts deep into the pocket, making sure you work both sides and the far back reaches.

Make a note that there are two ways to fish both points and pockets. Let's say the water at either spot is relatively deep (two to three feet, maybe). You can rig a popping or rattling cork about 18 inches deep and float a bait under it so that it rests just off the bottom. If, on the other hand, the water is shallow (or if you'd just prefer to "tightline" the bait), you can leave the cork off the rigging and simply cast and retrieve.

Both natural and artificial bait will work in points and pockets. Best natural baits include live shrimp, market shrimp, live baby crabs, live Cocahoe minnows, or pieces of cut squid or mullet. Best artificials run the gamut from split-tail beetles to plastic Cocahoe tails to grubs. Even a well-placed topwater plug, like a Mirrorlure or a Zara Spook, will provoke a strike (especially from an aggressive redfish).

Ordinarily, though, redfish and flounder will hit any of these baits and lures, either resting directly on the bottom or suspended under a cork. Drum will occasionally strike at them all but generally prefer the natural baits, either cast and retrieve or suspended under a cork. Of course, stingrays, as well, will strike mostly at the natural baits.

If you fish with artificials, tie the artificial directly to the monofilament. Do not use a swivel to attach any lure to the mono except silver or gold weedless spoons or the old Sidewinder. These metal baits need to be rigged so that they swivel and not twist the line—jig heads don't twist line so they don't need to be swiveled on. That old antiquated kinda stuff went out with Wizard Outboards and shad rigs. Good fishermen don't do that anymore!

For the most part, you can catch virtually any species that hangs out at the points and pockets with a quarter-ounce jig head. The only exception to this is the king- and queen-size plastic lures. Their larger size works better on a three-eighths- or half-ounce jig head.

And here's something else that might take you aback—the jig heads do not need to be painted! Plain, unpainted lead-head jigs, the round kind manufactured by H&H Lure Company out of Baton Rouge, for example, are all you really need. Everything else is gingerbread and overkill! It's more important that you learn to thread the plastic lure onto the jig head so that it is straight, runs true in the water, and doesn't swim off cockeyed when retrieved. Fish don't ever strike consistently at cockeyed lures!

Under a cork, you can go one of two ways—either (1) the jig head suspended or (2) a Kahle hook tied directly to a shock leader with a split-shot installed slightly above the hook eye to keep the bait submerged.

If you fish with natural baits, you can use a jig head tipped with a piece of market shrimp, baby crab, or live Cocahoe minnow. This procedure works for either bottom or suspended cork fishing. You can also use a Kahle hook on a Carolina rig, a Kahle hook freelined (that's just the hook tied to the monofilament with no weight whatsoever attached so that live bait can swim freely in the current), or a Kahle hook dangled under a popping or rattling cork with a live Cocahoe, live crab, live shrimp, or live croaker presented as "bait."

The methodology includes making the cast as close to the bank as possible (and making it as *quietly* as possible—it should not sound like a Buick falling off a car carrier!). Then, if you're fishing on the bottom, slowly retrieve the lure or bait in a short, twitching, erratic motion that will almost ensure a strike. Return the bait or lure back to the boat a little at a time. If twitchy retrieves don't produce strikes, then try a slow, steady retrieve. One or the other will surely work if you've successfully picked out a productive point or pocket.

If you're fishing under a cork, again throw the cork as close to the bank as possible. Then with an intermittent popping motion, slowly bring it back to the boat. Science has proven that if there are any fish in the area, and you're doing the presentation correctly, they should be on top of the bait or lure within the first six to eight pops. If they aren't, wind in and make another cast in another direction. Of course, sometimes you just have to let the cork rest, unpopped, especially when you're fishing live shrimp or minnows (sometimes that's how the fish want it!).

CHAPTER 35

Fishin' by the Numbers—Gospel 3

HOW TO FISH TROUT AND REDS AWAY FROM THE SHORELINE

So by now, after reading and rereading and digesting Gospels 1 and 2, you've got the hang of fishing for trout and redfish along the shoreline, right?

You know to move in just close enough to put you within casting range (even though you got to reach out a little). You know to approach as quietly as possible so you don't spook the fish. You know not to park on top of the fish (you know to read the fishing conditions as you approach and you know to decide right away whether you need to be situated off the bank fishing in, or right up on the bank fishing out).

You know how to rig the terminal tackle to keep the bait out of the shoreline snags. You know about twitching and jerking and steady retrieves (and when to use which). You know to look for congregating baitfish (and consequently the fish that will move in on them sooner or later). You know about fishing all the pockets and the points. You know about casting so close to the bank you actually "bruise" the grass. You know when it's time to work the popping or rattling cork and when it's time to just let it sit.

If you don't know all this, if all of this isn't yet like second nature to you, then stop right here and go back and read Gospels 1 and 2 again. Because in this chapter and verse the fishing spot changes; this time you're going to learn how to handle the fishing action when it takes place *away* from the shoreline.

Sometimes, maybe because of influencing weather systems, changing barometer, dirty water conditions caused by pounding surf, low water conditions caused by excessive tides, and a host of other reasons, trout and redfish will be holding "away from the shoreline," "out from the bank," "in the middle of the bay or pond." How do you decide that this is the case? Well, you first fish up against the shoreline; but if nothing happens, before you pick up and head for another spot, turn your back on the bank and make a significant number of casts in the opposite direction—*out from the bank.*

Remember, you and I really don't know what the underwater habitat is like up against the bank, and we have no concept of what makes up the environs 30, 40, and even 50 feet off the shoreline. Distanced off the bank could be a shelf, a drop-off, a hole, a reef, or any number of other topographical structures and contours made by the Maker to hold fish. So for that reason, when nothing happens along the bank, or when the bites suddenly stop, do a 180 and cast in the opposite direction: *work the middle!*

The techniques won't change all that much:

1. You still have to be quiet.

2. You still don't drop the anchor.

3. You still try the bottom (by fishing tightline), using the long cast, steady retrieve, then twitch, then jerk, or whatever it takes to provoke a hit.

4. If tightlining doesn't work, you still try the mid-depths by suspending the bait or lure 18 to 22 inches under a popping cork, popping it intermittently to churn up some interest, or simply letting it sit and drift in the current (because sometimes popping actually frightens the fish and chases them away).

5. And depending upon the season, you still use the same baits and lures you used to fish along the shoreline (live Cocahoes, baby croakers, live shrimp, market shrimp, plastic swimming tails,

artificial split-tail beetles, or whatever else "they" might seem to want).

It really isn't critical which type of tackle you use—*baitcasting or spincasting.* It is critical, however, that the rod and reel of your choice be in prime working condition (cleaned, oiled, filled with fresh line, and no broken guides). If you prefer to fish bait-casting gear, do it; if spincasting is your thing, no problem. I will tell you that I bring along both kinds and I fish with both kinds all day long on each and every trip. I bring out the baitcasting gear when I have the wind to my back or when there's not enough wind to influence my casts. But whenever I have to pitch into the wind, or whenever I want to fish "close quarters," I find it much easier to throw the spinning gear.

Fishing "away from the bank" requires more skill than fishing toward it. That's because your casts have no defined targets. Close to the bank you can pick out a point, or stump, or inden-tation in the marsh where you think there might be a fish hold-ing up; out in the middle, you just attempt to cover water. And that's why you need to practice a technique called "fancasting."

Fancasting is just what the name implies—if you could see an image of all your casts, the pattern would appear much like the arch and staves of a fan. And this is how the pro anglers cover all that open water!

From the back of the boat, say, cast 90 degrees straight off the stern. The next cast then should move a slight bit forward. The next shoots out at about a 45-degree angle, followed by the next one almost perpendicular to the side of the boat. The pattern continues until the final cast in "the fan" is practi-cally straight off the bow, nearly parallel to the boat.

You hear the guides forever talking about "covering water" and "staying in the strike zone." This is how it's done. You liter-ally have to pull the bait or lure through as much water volume as possible to increase your odds of pulling it in front of a fish! Then once you find out where the fish are, once you determine whether they want the bait played fast or slow, once you decide whether to keep it high or low in the water column, you've found the "zone where they will strike." From that moment on, you want to make every cast in the same place and play it exactly the same as the last one. The result? You'll catch fish!

Finally, a few Commandments for keeping the fish you hook, whether you hook them along the shoreline or out in open water:

• Never horse them back to the boat—keep the rod tip up and let the flexibility of the rod play the fish. Reel in when the fish comes to you; stop reeling when he runs away from you.

• Eliminate what is generally known as "hang time." When you have the fish almost to the gunwale of the boat, at which point there should be about four feet of line coming off the tip of the rod, stop reeling and simply "swing" the fish directly toward you, again using the flexibility of the rod to catapult the fish into your midsection. Avoid winding in too much line! Never try to wind the fish through the rod guides! And never ever let the fish dangle over the water! That's "hang time." Don't let him hang there—get him in the boat!

• If you have the slightest inkling that the fish is too hefty for the line, use the landing net. Don't try to lift him into the boat using the mono—you'll probably lose him.

• If you get a strike but miss the fish, go right back to the same spot and try him again. Unless you stick him hard with the hook, he'll probably come back for the bait a second time.

Drifting is always the ideal method for fishing open water. I never recommend you drop anchor unless you're drifting along and you suddenly get into a massive school of fish that takes down all the lines in the boat. At times like this, go ahead and ease the anchor over and see if the school is in "residence" or if it's "migrating." If it's in residence, you'll catch a full limit in less than 10 minutes; if it's migrating, the bites will stop after about the third cast as the fish move away.

CHAPTER 36

Fishin' by the Numbers—Gospel 4

TEASING WITH TOPWATERS

Tie on a "Top Dog," a "Zara Spook," a "Chug Bug," or any of a hundred other topwater floater baits. Twitch, jerk, and zigzag them across the ripples in simulated death throes. Trout will strike at them with a vengeance, inhaling sometimes three sets of treble hooks before spitting them out without so much as a scratch! Redfish will chase them across the surface of the water, snapping in pursuit like a junkyard dog on the heels of the mailman. But that's the kind of excitement you can experience only when topwater fishing!

Here's why it's so popular and enticing a technique:

1. Even as you sit on the gunwale of the boat to tie on the bait, you can sense the excitement. Your psyche knows that soon you'll cast this taunting inanimate object within provoking range of any fish that sees it. Your pulse will slightly quicken.

2. You are filled with anticipation as the lure darts and gyrates over the surface of the water, knowing that at any moment a trout or a red or a flounder could stealthily rise up under it and, in a single gulp, attempt to inhale it! Your pulse rate climbs even higher.

3. Adrenaline instantly surges through your body as your anticipation becomes staunch reality! You see the silvery flash of the big fish as it lurches halfway out of the water! You're startled by the trout's powerful onslaught shattering the water's surface tension! You're taken aback by the boiling surf as the big fish

195

attempts to devour the bait in one savage bite! And as your pulse speeds to racing level, you restrain the deep-seated urge to hurry and set the hook, unsure as to whether the fish has the treble sets in its jaws or is just sinking the bait with its body weight!

4. And when you do set the hook and you feel the solid run of the fish's power, knowing for certain that he's at the end of the line, your heart palpitates and you finally let loose the breath you've been unconsciously holding all this time, in a shout that can be heard at the next fishing hotspot one complete parish away!

Topwater fishing is like that, exactly like that! It involves fishing with almost all your senses. So to experience it fully, you really should learn to do it right. Here's how.

1. Select for your tackle only the highest-quality, brand-name topwater baits. Those cheapies you find on clearance counters at the sporting-goods stores won't do the job. Good topwater baits are engineered like scientific instruments to emulate real fish, to dance rhythmically, to float in balanced orchestration over the surface. To entice a monster trout to come to the surface like a Polaris missile takes the real thing!

2. Regardless of what kind of fishing you intend to do when you start out, be sure to always bring along your topwater lures *"just in case."* Just in case you notice some movement on the surface that piques your interest. Just in case you find an isolated pocket in the grassline that looks tempting to you. Just in case you notice that something appeared to strike at your jig head the last time you retrieved it across the top of the water, or that something snapped at your popping cork up on the surface the last time you popped it. These are definite indicators that you should immediately throw a topwater.

3. What color to throw? You'll have to experiment. All the pros do, too. Blue and silver, red and white, green and creme, orange and yellow—they all seem to work well on many occasions. But you'll need to have a good variety in your tackle box, because in the end the fish—*and only the fish!*—gets to make the final selection.

4. How to fish 'em? I prefer to fish topwaters on spinning rather than baitcasting tackle. Spinning gear allows you to cast farther (and even into the wind) with less backlash potential. In my estimation it also allows you to put more twitch, snap, zip, and twitter on the lure as it comes through the water. But if you are really proficient with baitcasting equipment, it too works well.

5. Always tie the lure directly to the line (either braided line or monofilament). Never use a snap swivel or even a split ring when fishing topwater baits—*it totally destroys the natural action the design engineers built into the lure.*

6. Make a long cast, lock down the bail, and then begin short "wrist-action" twitches, retrieving the lure as you go. Vary the twitch and retrieve too. Sometimes twitch once, sometimes twitch twice, and occasionally twitch several times. But the actual motion of the retrieve is the more critical action of the two. Unquestionably, the tactic requires ambidexterity—both the left and right hands need to work in harmony. If they don't, the pattern will probably fail to produce strikes with any consistency!

7. Of course, the most important virtue a topwater fisherman can possess is *patience.* Unlike bottom-fishing or tightlining, you never ever want to set the hook "on the strike." *Always, always* contain your emotions, exercise restraint, and count at least "two-Mississippi" before you rear back! This may very well turn out to be the most difficult task in the world. But it is imperative that you give the fish time to get a solid bite on the lure. Otherwise he's going to spit it and all of its treble hooks with the force of lava coming out of Mount Aetna.

Now pay close attention:

None of these techniques will be mastered overnight! Repetition is necessary. All require endless hours of practice to reach perfection. So don't become frustrated if at first you twitch and jerk and pop and twitter and you never catch a fish. Just follow all these directions and stay with it! Your reward is worth every second of the effort you put into it.

SPOONING THE PONDS

Fishing with a gold or silver spoon (gold is more popular) requires the same degree of dedication to technique as does fishing with topwater baits. But just as there are certain similarities, there are also noted differences.

1. Never buy the bargain-basement version of gold spoons! They have to be precision-forged pieces of metal; otherwise they will never look or behave like the swimming, flashy-sided baitfish they are supposed to mimic. Go for brand names— the price you pay will be justified by what you catch.

2. While you tie a topwater directly to the monofilament, you always, always tie a spoon to a swivel. You can use a high-quality snap swivel or you can use a split ring on a barrel swivel. *But use a swivel.* The device allows the metal to wobble properly without putting unforgivable twists in your line. Leave the swivel off and you'll spend all day long untangling line!

3. Where to fish spoons? And for what? Inshore, spoons are used primarily for redfish, but speckled trout and the occasional flounder seemingly have no aversion to chasing them down. You should tie one on and toss it whenever you find yourself drifting along the shoreline, especially if it's loaded with fish-holding structure and grass (remember to buy only weedless spoons). But they were initially forged by most of the major manufacturers to fish shallow-water ponds where bronzed-backed, bottom-grubbing, voracious reds forage through the thick grass mats in search of baitfish.

4. How to fish 'em? They come in three sizes (let's just call them small, medium, and large for the purpose of simplification), and this rule of thumb applies: "big bait, big fish." Which one you decide to tie on depends upon what size redfish are prowling the ponds. Make your cast (and learn to ease the spoon into the water, which eliminates the fish-spooking splash), then begin the retrieve. But here's what surprises most fishermen. Use a *steady retrieve*—no jerks, no twitches, no snaps. The guys at the plant who made the spoon built in it for you the kind of action it needed to have. You just cast it

and retrieve it. Oh, every now and then you can vary the speed of the retrieve for a little changeup, but for best results let the spoon do the work!

5. Finally, the same suggestion about setting the hook applies to the spoon that applies to the topwater bait. Most fish that strike the spoon will come up behind it, chase it down, and stop it in its tracks. Don't pull back the instant you feel the "bump." Let the fish swim away with his prize for a split second (again, "two-Mississippi" works well). Then set the hook so hard you cross his eyes!

Once more, I recommend you go back and read the first three gospels, absorbing the information like a sponge. Then reread this gospel, all before you make your next trip. I don't guarantee you'll catch a full limit of trout, reds, and flounders next time you head out, but I do promise you that you'll shift the odds of success in your favor!

CHAPTER 37

Fishin' by the Numbers—Gospel 5

FINDIN' AND FISHIN' FOR FLOUNDERS

They're technically known as flatfish. They swim horizontally instead of vertically. They have both eyes located on the same side of the head. They feed on their prey from an ambush position. They're anything but eager to give up the fight when they're hooked. And they're worth hooking because they're outstanding as table fare fixed in any number of ways. By now I guess you know I'm talking about flounders.

There was a time when you caught flounders along Southern Louisiana primarily in the summertime. But then all of a sudden it seemed something happened. The coastal ecology must have changed, because now they're in our waters almost every month of the year and you can catch them if you know the right techniques.

First and foremost, learn the biology of the species. If you don't understand its traits, habits, and characteristics, you'll never catch it except by accident. Most important of all is to realize that because of the way it is designed, the flounder isn't one of those fish that can eye its prey, then chase it down at breakneck speed.

Because it is what's called a "flatfish," it must swim on its side, horizontally, instead of vertically like most other fish. That limitation in itself makes for a difficult task in pursuing and attacking its dinner. But that's where biological adaptation comes in.

When it is in deep, open water, the flounder lies flat on the bottom and rapidly undulates its fins to barely cover its body with mud, silt, or sand. When in extremely shallow water along the bank—which is its most preferred habitat—the fish almost buries itself completely, save for its eyes and mouth. This is the ambush "setup."

Depending upon the current, the movement of the tide, and the wind-induced wave action hitting the shoreline, the flounder could be laying either parallel to the bank, pointed to the bank, or pointed away from the bank. This is its attack posture. *Facing the bank,* it can make easy meals out of extremely small baitfish swimming the shoreline and attempting to hide in the marsh root system. *Facing away from the bank,* it can surge forward in a stealth attack from behind to take deeper-swimming prey or prey swimming away from the shoreline grasses. The flounder always lies *parallel to the bank* when it takes up position on either side of a point, where parallel-moving currents push baitfish uncontrollably around the point and into its waiting jaws.

So what does all this have to do with being able to catch a mess of flounder? Plenty. It dictates exactly how you should fish for them. And unless you fish for them appropriately, you can bet your Cajun mud anchor that you'll catch flounder only accidentally! Here's the procedure:

1. Fish on the bottom—flat on the bottom! The flounder is on the bottom, right? You should put the bait you plan to use on the bottom with him.

2. Fish slow, slow, slow! Remember how I said that flounders just aren't built for chasing food at breakneck speed? Not only are they not built for it, they just don't do it as a matter of principle! If you want to catch flounder, you will have to "slowly" drag the bait over the fish or at least close enough to him to entice him to move forward in a quick thrust to snap at it! Move the bait too fast and the fish will just stay put until something easier comes along.

3. Two methods of terminal rigging work best for flounders—

quarter-ounce jig head on the bottom or quarter-ounce Carolina rig. The "jig head on the bottom" tactic will work with both natural and artificial baits. The Carolina rig is best used for live or market bait.

4. Regardless of which tackle configuration you prefer, make the cast and allow the rigging to settle on the bottom. Then ever so slowly, using short, snappy, miniature jerks and twitches, work the rigging back to the boat. Up against a grassline, cast so close to the bank that you actually bruise the bushes. In open water, leave the bail open until you're absolutely certain you're flat on the bottom. Wherever you're fishing, just keep telling yourself the whole time, "This is a mean fish, but this is one damn lazy fish!"

5. Know what the bite will feel like! This is critical. So many fishermen get flounder bites and never know it. Don't expect one of those "freight-train, slash-and-run, rip-the-rod-out-of-your-hand" kinda bites. Right now, say the word "boomp!" That's the average flounder bite. Take the index finger on your right hand and quickly tap it once on the backside of your left hand. Feel that? That's a *vicious* flounder bite! The more subtle bite often appears to be nothing more than a "snag on the bottom," which means that it's possible that all those times you thought you where hung up on grass on the bottom . . . oh, well, now you know!

6. Flounders are equipped with a set of teeth than can handle almost anything edible. So it's possible that they'll bite whatever you happen to be fishing with. Their preferences, however, are—*in this order*—live shrimp, live minnows, live baby croakers, market shrimp, and, yes, even artificials, particularly the clear glitter-sparkled beetle, the glow-in-the-dark grub, the avocado- or motor-oil-colored splittail beetle, and the old reliable standby smoke-glitter Cocahoe tail.

7. Let me see if I can describe one particularly effective technique I've always used when fishing specifically for flounders. Whether you're shallow up against the grass or deep in the middle of Lake Pontchartrain, make your cast. Then after

the rigging has settled to the bottom, simply lift the rod tip to 11 o'clock and then momentarily hold it there, waiting and concentrating and sensing for vibrations in the line. Then, after about two or three seconds, gently drop the rod tip back to nine o'clock (essentially parallel to the water's surface), take up the slack, and repeat the process. If at any time during this procedure you feel that "boomp" we talked about earlier, *set the hook!*

Finally, keep steady line pressure on a flounder (the fish is strong and can quickly throw a hook). Don't ever try to horse him to the boat or you run the risk of losing him. And whenever possible, use a landing net to bring him aboard.

Oh, one more thing. Flounders can be filleted and fixed any way you like them—fried, baked, broiled, grilled, bronzed, blackened, steamed, or smoked. But one of the best ways to fix them is to scale and gut them (scaling is a tad time consuming, but the old aluminum toothed scraper always works best) and prepare them whole.

An oven-baked or broiled flounder stuffed with crabmeat and slathered with lemon-butter sauce is death-row gourmet! And small flounders scaled and gutted, scored diagonally over the tops and bottoms, dipped in Frank Davis Fish Fry, deep-fried to crunchy perfection, and served for two by candlelight with glasses of chilled white wine are known as "love fish." Just this recipe and presentation alone make studying all this material about flounders worth whatever time it took!

And as Forrest Gump would say, "And that's all I have to say about that!"

CHAPTER 38

Fishin' by the Numbers—Gospel 6

CATCHIN' PUPPY DRUM

Remember chapter 4 about sheepshead? Make one or two changes and you have everything you need to know about fishing for drum. Changes like:

• Instead of looking for pilings and bridge supports, look for oyster beds and deep holes where drum can congregate in schools and "grub" their way along the bottom. That's where you want to fish.

• Their favorite foods are almost the same as those preferred by the sheepshead, only they can't rip and chew barnacles off pilings—their mouths are not designed for that. Nevertheless, whatever they can wrap their lips around down on the bottom becomes crushed fodder very quickly in the "grinders" located in the back of their throats.

• Use the same terminal tackle for drum that you use for sheepshead if you want consistent catches. They will try to eat artificials like split-tail beetles every now and then (probably because they perceive them to be shrimp), but market bait and pieces of cracked crab are prime baits. There's an old saying that goes, "A drum will cross a busy interstate at drive time to get to a piece of crab!" I've never been able to dispute that.

Now you will find some areas in Louisiana and Mississippi where "bull drum" lurk—these are the big 30-, 40-, and 50-pound giants. If you happen to hook into one of them at some point, be sure to release it unharmed. It's almost a certainty it will be overloaded with white worms and it'll be as tough as the tongue and side-leather on a pair of combat boots.

The drum you really want are what fishermen refer to as "puppy drum." These are the little fish that are "right at legal size"—16 inches exactly. Their fillets are flaky, light, white, and relatively free of worms. They also have a minimum bloodline, which you should always trim away. Oh, and don't forget that unlike the sheepshead, drum do have a creel limit—five fish per person per day (just like reds).

So now that you know all this, if all you still ever want to fish for are trout and reds, that's okay. Leave the drum for me!

CHAPTER 39

Fishin' by the Numbers—Gospel 7

COMMON QUERIES

I'm kneeling in church one Sunday morning at 8:30 mass, head bowed in silent prayer, watching out of the corner of my eye as the faithful parade past me up to the altar for Holy Communion.

Suddenly, as unexpected as a nuclear flash, there's this husky voice in my left ear. I jump with a start and totally forget the second half of the Hail Mary I was saying.

"Frank, wanna ask ya . . . what does it mean to 'sweeten the bait'?" the man mumbles in a strained whisper, stooping low to talk with me in the pew. Then, being forced forward by the movement of the communion line, he turns back briefly and says, "Never mind right now—you can tell me after church!"

I guess no matter where the questions are posed, as the slogan for the checkout-counter scandal paper proclaims, "Inquiring minds want to know!" And that obviously includes questions from the minds of fishermen! That being the case, this gospel is going to answer some questions. Let's pick up with the one asked in church.

Q. What does it mean to "sweeten the bait"?

A. To "sweeten" a bait means you add a little tidbit of some natural bait to an artificial lure to give it flavor and scent. For example, if you were fishing with a smoke-colored split-tail beetle on a quarter-ounce jig head, you'd "sweeten" that up by tipping the hook with a small piece of market shrimp. If you were fishing with a gold spoon, you would "sweeten" it up by adding a real Cocahoe minnow to the weedless hook (even a dead minnow would do). So simply add a pinch of some natural bait to an artificial bait, and the artificial is "sweetened."

Q. What's the bite from a redfish or flounder really going to feel like when you're fishing a jig head and plastic Cocahoe tail along the shoreline?

A. The question you asked is actually two questions in one—(1) what's a redfish bite feel like, and (2) what's a flounder bite feel like? Actually it's really two different bites. You'll sense the redfish strike as a "heavy, solid thump," almost as if someone had dropped a brick on your line. The flounder bite comes off much subtler, kinda like someone took their index finger and flicked the lure (imagine what it would be like to flick a popcorn kernel off your kitchen table onto the floor).

The redfish bite usually maintains significant tension on your line because the fish will ordinarily swim parallel to your boat and the bank; therefore the hook will be rather simple to set. The flounder bite, however, usually produces excess slack in your line because the fish ordinarily swims perpendicular to your boat and away from the bank. If you don't instantly take up the slack and set the hook, you'll almost always lose a flounder.

Q. I lose a lot of big fish that swim under my boat and break off. Is there any way to keep this from happening?

A. A fish, especially a big fish, is going to swim wherever he wants to and there is brave little you and I can do to keep him from doing so. We can, however, prevent him from breaking the line—*sometimes*—on those power runs under the boat and around the outboard. Try this: the next time you bring a hawg up toward the boat and he plows his way under it, instead of horsing him to keep him from running, thereby putting undue stress on your monofilament, instead plunge the rod tip into the water vertically (all the way up to the reel if you have to!) so that the fish is forced to fight low, well below the propeller on the outboard and the barnacles on the keel. Don't be afraid to get your tackle wet—it's saved a lot of would-be-lost fish records.

Q. I want to know why in God's name we always gotta get up and get out on the water so dad-gummed early in the morning just to catch fish. What is it about these fish eating breakfast?

A. You really *don't* have to get up early in the morning to catch fish. But you do have to get up early in the morning to "catch the tide moving just right"! At least, most of the time, anyway. Actually, it's not "breakfast" you need to be concerned with—that's only coincidental. It just so happens that on this planet Earth, we usually have our best tidal activity early in the morning hours, which almost independently dictates whether the fishing will be good or not. Keeping that in mind, then, let's say you'd really like to "sleep in" one morning, fish later in the day, and yet still be guaranteed relatively good fishing conditions. Then forget about checking the clock; check the tidal charts instead. Plan to fish when the tides are moving at their best, regardless of whether they are incoming or outgoing. (Oh, yeah—the same holds true for fishing after work. Just "go fishin'" if your intent is only to get out for a while; but check the tides before you go if your intent is to *catch* fish.)

Q. I try to fish under the seagulls the way you pros tell me to do, but I see them diving all over the place and I ain't never caught a thing fishing like this. What am I not understanding?

A. You got to fish the right kind of gulls! No kidding. The large common seagulls that cluster in feeding flocks and dive into the water are the ones that are genuinely feeding on debris regurgitated by schools of fish under the surface. These are the birds you look for; these are the birds that literally squeal out as if saying, *"Fish here!"* And then there is the species that Capt. Phil Robichaux likes to refer to as "lying gulls." These are smaller birds that sort of glide and hover just over the surface of the water, occasionally dipping downward to sample the ripples yet never truly diving. These birds generally pick up small migrating baitfish that accidentally happen to cruise too close to the surface. Generally, there are no feeding fish under them. So if you're going to "fish the birds," you gotta fish the right ones.

Q. If I'm using a popping cork and I see it go under, when, exactly, do I set the hook? I seem to miss a whole lot of fish fishing this way.

A. Lots of fishermen miss a lot of fish fishing with a cork. And there is, indeed, a proper methodology, whether you're using live bait, market bait, or artificials. Here's how it should be done:

1. Make the cast.
2. Let the cork settle in the water.
3. Pick up all the slack that might develop in your line.
4. Pop the cork moderately hard, occasionally, to froth the water surface (this emulates the sound of a fish feeding on the surface and is intended to interest other fish nearby).
5. Stop popping the cork altogether and let it just sit on the water if you notice that popping it seems to be spooking the fish (this does happen sometimes!).
6. When the strike comes and the cork submerges, do *not* set the hook immediately, especially if you're using live shrimp, live Cocahoes, or live croakers (you must give the fish time to turn the bait in its mouth so that the hook and barb are pointed in the right direction).
7. Wait until the line straightens out, wait until all the slack is taken up, and wait until you can actually feel the tension on the monofilament.
8. At this point, and only at this point, lean slightly forward to anchor the hook-set, thereby horizontally pointing the entire rod at the running fish.

9. And then . . . *you pull back,* raising the rod tip to 12 o'clock high, freezing it there for a second or two, and giving the fish absolutely no slack, all the way back to the boat.

Fish 'em this way and you'll miss a few once in a while, but you won't miss very many!

Q. Everybody keeps saying, "The croakers are back!" I love these little fish. So could you please tell me precisely where they are and what is the best method for catching them?

A. The croakers *are* back—and they're thick! For a long time, maybe 25 years, it was tough finding the little panfish (nobody really knows why, but salt barrels used by shrimpers were believed to have been the cause). But then they started showing up again at some of the more popular Southeast Louisiana hotspots—Delacroix, Shell Beach, Lafitte, the Lower Barataria, Hopedale, Irish Bayou, both the north and south shores of Lake Pontchartrain, and even along the New Orleans seawall. And the overall size is increasing, too.

I've named the spots where the biggest concentrations are located, but specifically they're bottom fish and will be clustered together primarily in deep holes, canals, and bayous and adjacent to structures in open water. You should fish them flat on the bottom using either a shortened Carolina rig (which means the leader should only be about 10 inches long), a jig head tied directly to the monofilament, or a single drop rig where the teardrop sinker rests on the bottom and the drop leader and hook are tied on about four to six inches above it.

They're a feisty, aggressive, adversarial kind of fish (which means they'll give you a tussle once you've snagged them). They prefer both live and market shrimp above all other baits, but they won't turn their noses up at squid or cut fish (even pieces of cut-up croaker or white trout).

Here's your technique:

Make your cast, let the bait settle to the bottom, then take all of the slack out of your line and get ready. When croakers bite, you have to stick 'em on the first shot; otherwise they'll clean the hook slicker than a whistle without giving you a second chance. Light tackle, 10-12-pound-test line, and a good drag set are all you really need to fill an ice chest full of them. They're outstanding scaled and gutted and fried whole! And there's no size limit or creel.

Q. What's the proper way to drift-fish? And when do you use this technique?

A. Drift-fishing is just what the name implies—there is no anchor, no pipe stuck in the ground, no nothing to hold the boat in one place. It simply drifts with either the wind or the tide and the primary purpose is to help you find schools and clusters of fish. But there is a methodical way to do it:

In a bayou or canal, slowly head upstream *against* the tide to the point where you want to begin fishing; then position the boat dead center in the bayou or canal and drift downstream with the tide (or the wind), casting against the shoreline on both sides of the drift. In a pond or lagoon, follow the shoreline so as not to spook or disturb the fish out in the middle. Then position the boat upwind so that the wind is at your back and pushes you across the pond, and cast on each side of the drift.

The best ways to fish when drift-fishing are either under a popping cork or cast and retrieve. Fishing on the bottom with a drop rig or Carolina rig should be avoided because of the possibility of snags.

Q. How long should I stay in one spot before packing up and moving?

A. Generally, when you arrive at a "fresh" spot, you will either begin catching fish immediately or catch them within 10 minutes. A good thick raft of fish (trout, reds, flounders, sheepshead, drum, and croakers) will begin biting right away and sometimes even before you shut off the outboard. Sometimes, though, the noise and ruckus of the engine will temporarily spook and scatter the fish, so it will take five or 10 minutes for them to return to the original spot and resume feeding. If, however, you coast up to a spot and you get nothing, zip, nada, zero, then within 10 minutes . . . find another location! *In fact, never never stay in an unproductive spot for more than 15 minutes!*

Q. I got some favorite artificials and for the most part I like to fish with them. But I really prefer to fish live bait. The problem is I never know how much is the right amount to bring along on a trip. Is there a scientific formula?

A. A formula? Well, kinda. As a general rule of thumb, if you're fishing with live shrimp you will want to bring along approximately 50 live shrimp per person. The renowned Kenny Campo explains that this is because you lose a lot of live shrimp in a lot of different ways—needlefish cut them off, catfish and pinfish steal them, crabs snip them in two, and they fly off the hook lots of times on a bad cast. Kenny says he always brings along 50 per person then adds a 50-shrimp buffer. It's usually enough for a full day on the water.

On the other hand, the Cocahoe minnow number is generally about half that of live shrimp. You don't throw them off the hook, you don't lose them that often to trash fish, and they have a higher catch ratio than shrimp. You should figure 30 Cocahoes per person with a 30-fish buffer and you should be just fine.

Q. What is the correct definition of "cut bait"? And what is "market bait"?

A. *Cut bait,* technically, is any species of fish (but usually mullet, croaker, shad, pogey, white trout, and even squid) cut into strips or small bite-size chunks that can be threaded onto a hook. Cut bait is primarily used for offshore-rig fishing, but sometimes for bull-red fishing on the whitewater breakers or along a deepwater shoreline.

Market bait, on the other hand, is generally a synonym for *dead shrimp* bought by the pound at the marina or fish market.

Occasionally, finger mullet, gizzard shad, and squid will be referred to as market bait. But that's a stretch!

Q. Frank, I like to make my own shock leaders, but I can never keep them separated and they're forever getting tangled up and knotted. Any suggestions?

A. Not only do I have a suggestion for you, I've got the perfect solution for you. You know those neat little bank envelopes you get at your favorite lending institution? The ones with the pressure-sensitive flap at the top? Well, see if you can talk the teller out of a box of them (or at least a big ol' stack!). Then take each leader you make, wind it in a coil, slip it down inside the envelope, and seal the flap. Then on the outside of the envelope write a brief description of whatever is inside (e.g., *Redfish Shock Leader/25#-Test Mono/18" Long/Barrel Swivels/1/4-oz. Leadhead Jig*, or *Carolina Rig/20" Long/Bronze Swivel/Straight 6/0 Mustad Hook*).

Then the next time you're out fishing and you need a leader, all you do is go into your tackle box and find the envelope that contains the kind of leader you want. All you do is tear off the top of the envelope, pop the rigging out, uncoil the mono, and tie it on your line. No fuss, no muss, no tangles, and no profanities! (Oh, yeah, you can keep all the envelopes organized and in one place in your tackle box simply by putting a rubber band around them.) Easy, huh?

Q. I'm never sure how much tackle to bring with me on a fishing trip. It seems that whenever I leave some of it home, that's the stuff I need to catch 'em with! And if I bring it all, there are four and five tackle boxes aboard! Help me out, would you?

A. I must admit that your problem was also my problem (and lots of fishermen's problem), or at least it was until recently. I was actually getting a hernia carrying five—*yes, five!*—tackle boxes aboard! It was too much, I knew, but I didn't know how to leave anything that I might need behind.

Then I remembered that 21st-century word everyone is using these days—*downsizing!* So I went to my favorite department store and bought a multicompartment canvas zipper bag and a box of pint-size Zip-Locs. I then made up bags containing one or two of my favorite hard-plastic lures, a dozen or so quarter-ounce and half-ounce jig heads, a dozen or so plastic tails in a variety of the colors I know work, a handful of quarter-ounce egg sinkers to use on my Carolina rigs, about 10 to 12 Kahle hooks in various sizes, maybe four or five popping corks, a short stack of those bank envelopes with my leaders in them, and probably three or four weedless spoons.

Additionally, in the most easily accessible compartment, I put a pair of needlenose pliers or a hook remover, a pair of snips for cutting monofilament (this could be a pair of toenail clippers, preferably on a lanyard), a pair of sunglasses, a disposable camera, my hand-held GPS unit, a few rattling corks, one of those clawlike fish grabbers, and a really sharp, short-blade filleting knife. Oh, yeah—I also threw in a can of bug spray and a fishing towel.

I promise you, if you do this you will have with you essentially every kind of fishing tackle you could ever need, and you will have eliminated four monster tackle boxes. So okay, maybe you really would like to have tied on the Appaloosa Pink Topwater Slugger Stallion Chugger With the Purple Polka Dots and Tiger Stripes, but, heck, that old smoke grub under the popping cork catches just as many big trout. And your hernia is slowly going away, too!

Q. My neighbor talks about "spooking redfish." I don't want to sound stupid to him so I never ask him what it means. But what does it mean?

A. Characteristically, redfish are a very wary species. So the slightest disturbance in the water, the most hardly noticeable splash, or even a muted noise in the bottom of the boat all scare the bejabers out of redfish. And all this is amplified tenfold when the redfish are in extremely shallow or clear water.

The old-timers used to say, "You gotta be really, really quiet if you wanna be a redfisherman!" Lately, the general fishing populace seems to have gotten away from that. But I can tell you without fear of contradiction that quiet fishermen will always catch more redfish, easier and faster, than noisy fishermen. Because they don't spook the fish! And the bottom line is . . . *spooked redfish won't bite!*

So how do you avoid spooking reds? Well, you *ease* into the shoreline where they're feeding—you don't run right up to it at full throttle. You use the trolling motor or the wind to drift a bank, flat, or oyster reef—you don't splash up the water with paddles or oars. You gently sneak the anchor into the water at a spot you want to fish—you don't "throw" the anchor overboard. And you don't slam ice-chest lids, bang the anchor chain on the floor of the boat, drop the tackle box, and play jackhammer rock-and-roll songs on the boom box you installed in the console. Because all of that spooks the fish and the bottom line is . . . *spooked fish won't bite!*

Q. On the subject of redfish, Frank, some folks say they can see them in the water. I've never seen them. Maybe I just don't know what to look for—what do you look for?

A. Sight-fishing is an important technique to learn if you want to catch fish consistently. There are several ways to "see" redfish. First you can sometimes see violent splashes along the shoreline, usually right alongside the grass. These are reds voraciously feeding on shrimp, crabs, and mullets. Then you can sometimes see their entire backs (and sometimes their tails) sticking above the surface of the water. This is referred to as "finning" or "tailing." And finally, you can sometimes see them cruising the shoreline flats. This appears as a "torpedo-type wake" and usually occurs when the fish is startled or spooked.

Splashing fish, finning fish, and tailing fish, if approached very quietly with a lot of stealth, can be caught by casting to them and presenting the bait in an enticing manner. But torpedoing fish can be caught only when they're first observed.

Once they're spooked and break into a "full wake," you can usually write them off.

Q. Some fishing reports I read say popping a cork briskly attracts trout and redfish—others say that popping the cork doesn't do anything but spook the fish. What's the real story here?

A. Actually, both statements are correct. It all depends on the fishing conditions, the location, and the circumstances. You gotta remember that the primary reason for the use of a cork in the first place is not to *attract* fish—that's lagniappe. The cork is a device that suspends the bait in the water column and keeps it off the bottom. But even more significant, if you've set the depth correctly, the cork should put the bait or lure smack-dab into the fish's feeding zone.

Sometimes you'll catch all the fish you can stand just by letting the cork float lazily on the surface—at times like this the fish just seem to be able to find the bait no matter what. There are even times when, possibly because the fish are agitated, popping the cork will just cause them to turn tail and run. But then there are those times, especially for redfish along the bank, when you just have to pop the cork and pop it really hard to grab the red's attention. Then again, sometimes if you pop the cork in really shallow water, you'll scare the bejabers out of the redfish and down the bank he goes (and these explanations hold true whether you fish with live bait or artificials). Some fishermen believe you don't ever have to pop a cork if you're using live shrimp or live Cocahoes. In all my years on the water, I've never found that to be a tried-and-true rule—sometimes you pop, sometimes you don't.

So you can see for yourself, "to pop or not to pop," well, it all depends. I recommend you try it both ways and see what works at any given time. You'll be able to tell!

Q. I hear some of the guys in the sportsman's league talking about "double anchoring." Exactly what is it and what does it do to help you catch more fish?

A. "Double anchoring" is the technique of anchoring both the bow and the stern of the boat to prevent it from swinging in the tide or current. It works best when the fish are striking in one particular spot that is difficult to reach by everyone in the boat (assuming the boat swings perpendicular to the spot). Under these conditions, fishing becomes easier if you position the boat parallel to the spot using two anchors, so that every fisherman will be casting out of the side of the boat to the fish.

Q. What's a "snelled" hook and why would you want to use one?

A. A hook that is snelled is one where the attached monofilament leader is wrapped in coils around the shank of the hook instead of being attached to the hook eye. It originally was designed to place the barb in direct line with the leader, thereby aiding "meat fishermen" by greatly improving the hooking qualities. Snelled hooks were really popular in the past with anglers who used natural bait, but sportfishermen generally stopped using them in the belief that the bulky wraps made the hook more visible to the fish.

No doubt about it, line strength is maximized when a hook is snelled; but today they are used primarily by bottom-fishermen out after more aggressive species, like drum, croaker, jack crevalle, amberjack, tuna, cobia, and gafftops. They are also still extensively used on trotlines for catfishing.

I still snell my hooks whenever I fish live Cocahoes or market shrimp for flounders, drum, and redfish. I can't tell you why, other than I've always done it and it works for me.

Oh, yeah—everyone who has ever learned how to snell has done so on those rainy Saturday afternoons at the kitchen table. So watch the weather reports!

Q. Okay, Frank, once and for all, tell me the real deal on white trout. Why is everyone in such a hurry to throw them back? Too mushy? Full of worms? Hard to clean? What?

A. Actually, it's a lack of understanding of the species. Both the *white trout* (whose proper name is sand trout or common weakfish) and the *speckled trout* (whose proper name is spotted weakfish) belong to the same family—the *croaker* family. Both white trout and speckled trout occupy canals, reefs, and open bays, they both feed on market shrimp as well as live bait, and they both battle equally as fierce when hooked. The only difference between the two is at the table—the speckled trout has a slightly firmer flesh than its cousin. But guess how you, now as the learned fisherman, overcome that?

Once you figure out that you're into the white trout, you immediately begin adding water to the ice in your ice chest to form a *slush*. Then, as each white trout is brought aboard, you stop and immediately drop it into the slush, thereby chilling the fish instantly and consequently keeping its flesh firm.

Next, the moment you get back to the house, you fillet the fish while they are still cold and place the fillets in an ice-water bath (as opposed to into a pile on the cutting table). Then, set aside those you plan to use for supper and immediately pack the rest into heavy plastic bags. Fill the bags with water and stash them away in the freezer. Handle white trout this way and no one will be able to tell you they aren't the same table quality as "specks."

But here's the lagniappe! Sure, you can fry or grill or pan-sauté white trout fillets—and they're delicious. But do you remember those old-fashioned "codfish balls" Momma and MawMaw used to make for us on Fridays out of the canned Gorton's Fish Flakes? Well, first, you can't by the fish flakes any longer. But you shouldn't really care. Because nothing the Gorton's fishermen ever took out of the sea at Gloucester could ever compare to "Friday fish patties" made with flaked white trout! You think I'm kidding? Dig out your old recipe. Or call MawMaw on the phone and ask her for it. Then take out the white trout!

CHAPTER 40

Fishin' by the Numbers— Apostolic Quiz

Read each question carefully. Then select the correct answer from the multiple choices. See the end of the chapter for the answer key.

1. To improve your proficiency at sportfishing, you should devote a significant amount of time to
   a. Watching Jimmy Houston every Saturday morning on cable.
   b. Buying every imaginable color of Helicopter lure you can find.
   c. Hanging out at the marinas and talking only to the guys with bay boats.
   d. Studying as much as you can about fish biology and fishing techniques in the areas you plan to fish.

2. Fishing "the inside" literally means
   a. Casting from inside the screen porch at the camp into the canal.
   b. Fishing protected waters such as bayous, canals, ponds, and lagoons on the marsh.
   c. Having inside, privileged information about where the bigger fish are being caught.
   d. "Armchair fishing" by guys who want to get out on the water but hardly ever do.

3. One of the best ways to find feeding fish stacked up is to
   a. Look for flocks of seagulls diving.
   b. Look for a virtual armada of boats clustered in one area.
   c. Look for a shiny "slick" on the surface of the water.
   d. All of the above.

4. A true "slick" on the water
   a. Is where a slob fisherman dumped his bilge.
   b. Is where trout, reds, or other fish are actively feeding on bait fish.
   c. Is where a shiny spot, caused by clouds blocking the sunlight, forms on the water.
   d. Is a sign that someone who fished the spot earlier was obviously seasick.
5. "Fishing the birds" means
   a. Drifting into a flock of feeding seagulls and casting for fish congregated under them.
   b. Setting out crackers on the water to attract the gulls and then sneaking up with a cast net.
   c. Baiting your crab traps with "birds" (fisherman slang for various chicken parts).
   d. Running your outboard back and forth through flocks of seagulls to stir up fish schools.
6. The most popular terminal rigging for trout and redfish is
   a. A QB-15 Bingo tied to leadcore line.
   b. A quarter-ounce unpainted leadhead jig fitted with a chartreuse or smoke Cocahoe minnow.
   c. A half-ounce teardrop sinker tied to the monofilament just above a tied-on 6/0 hook.
   d. A Kahle hook tied directly to the monofilament and baited with market shrimp.
7. Gold spoons are used primarily for
   a. Fishing Spanish mackerel offshore.
   b. Fishing when the wind is in your face and you need extra weight to cast farther.
   c. Fishing for bronzeback redfish in grassy shallow-water ponds and lagoons.
   d. Fishing for bull drum in murky water.
8. In spite of what you might have heard, trolling motors
   a. Actually increase your chances of finding fish by allowing you to move with the schools.

b. Are really too costly to be put on boats fishing nothing but shallow-water ponds.

c. Should be used only to move the boat from one point to another, and not during actual fishing.

d. Create substantial vibrations in the water to attract fish.

9. Good places to find trout, redfish, and flounder on the marsh are

a. Over oyster reefs in early summer.

b. On points that jut off the grassy shoreline during the spring and fall.

c. In dead-end canals once winter chills set in.

d. All of the above.

10. You can identify drum and redfish feeding along the shoreline when

a. You notice their dorsal and tail fins protruding from the shallow water.

b. You see torpedo-like wakes racing along the bank.

c. Thick foam mats float to the surface where they churned up the water.

d. You actually hear them crunching oyster and clamshells on the bottom.

11. When you cast toward the shoreline, you should always

a. First cast on top of the grass and then slowly ease the lure into the water.

b. Use a popping cork to keep from getting hung up and losing tackle.

c. Cast as close to the grass as possible then work the bait slowly back to the boat.

d. Use either gold spoons or topwater lures to add extra action to the cast.

12. Which of the following is not considered a productive speckled-trout bait?

a. Live shrimp

b. Live baby croaker

    c. The chartreuse split-tail beetle

    d. A live fiddler crab

13. A Carolina rig is best described as

    a. A double-drop bottom rig manufactured in Raleigh, North Carolina for catfish.

    b. A terminal rigging where a sliding sinker is positioned to stop about 18 inches above a shock leader and the hook below it.

    c. A half-ounce jig head tied directly to the terminal end of the monofilament and baited with squid or market shrimp.

    d. A single Eagle Claw treble hook tied onto the monofilament without any weight whatsoever.

14. Popping corks or rattling corks catch more fish

    a. When skies are unusually cloudy.

    b. When fish are suspended at a specific feeding level.

    c. Because most fish have poor vision and must rely on some kind of disturbance on the surface to find their prey.

    d. Only on charter boats during the summer shrimp run.

15. To become a better fisherman, you must master

    a. The Macarena.

    b. Chug-bugging techniques.

    c. Twitching and jerking and "bruising the grass."

    d. Molding your own plastic baits.

16. When you fish with popping corks

    a. You must continually pop the cork to raise a ruckus on the surface.

    b. Sometimes you must "just let it sit," since sometimes the popping actually frightens the fish and chases them away.

    c. You should use them only on spincast equipment.

    d. You need a special "corking license" from the Wildlife and Fisheries Department.

17. Which rod and reel is best for casting against the wind?

    a. Spinning

    b. Baitcasting

    c. Side-chunking

    d. None of the above

18. The procedure preferred most by Southeast Louisiana fishermen to fight seasickness is
   a. Two raw eggs in a glass of orange juice before getting on the boat.
   b. Eight ounces of buttermilk, three aspirins, and a pork-chop sandwich at sunup.
   c. One TripTone upon rising and another one an hour later.
   d. Two Dramamine placed under the tongue after each time you throw up!

19. You should always use a landing net
   a. Whenever you catch fish over 12 inches long.
   b. Whenever there's a question as to the weight of the fish versus the pound test of the line.
   c. When you fish with your wife or girlfriend, 'cuz you'll never hear the end of it if you lose the fish overboard!
   d. When catching gafftops and eels.

20. If you miss a strike on a tightline retrieve, you should
   a. Pull anchor and haul it out of there before your friends find out!
   b. Hurry up and cast right back in the same area to give the fish a second opportunity to strike.
   c. Stop tightlining and use a rattling cork to alleviate any undue stress on the fish.
   d. Immediately enroll in a "Fishing for Dummies" class.

21. Live Cocahoe minnows should be hooked
   a. Through the tail fins.
   b. Through the eyes.
   c. Through the lips.
   d. In that soft spot under the gills.

22. Regardless of the kind of fishing you plan to do, always
   a. Bring along your topwater lures "just in case."
   b. Make sure you got extra drinks and sandwiches for those slack times when nothing is biting.
   c. Take a real novice with you so that you can show off a little when you catch most of the fish.
   d. Lie about where you've been when you get back to the dock.

23. Most flounders are found
   a. In the Mrs. Paul's frozen-food cases at Winn-Dixie.
   b. Hiding in ambush behind the leading edge of a point on the marsh.
   c. Sleeping upside-down on their backs during daylight hours on shell banks.
   d. Clustered under the rig stanchions about five miles off the coast of Grand Isle.

24. The proper technique to use when a big speckled trout picks up a live croaker off the bottom is
   a. Set the hook immediately so the fish won't be able to escape.
   b. Don't set the hook—just gently wind the reel so that you won't scare the trout.
   c. Hoop and holler at the top of your lungs to let other fishermen nearby know what you got!
   d. Resist the urge to set the hook immediately and give the trout time to take the croaker.

25. Regardless of whether you fish inshore, offshore, in fresh or salt water, it is always best to
   a. Use the heaviest tackle you can find to keep whatever you catch from getting away.
   b. Use the lightest tackle possible for the task since it provides you with the subtlest sensations of anything that bites.
   c. Buy generic equipment instead of brand names since fishing tackle breaks so easily.
   d. Fish around midday instead of early morning or late evening so that all the rookies will be out of your way by the time you arrive.

Now check your answers and total up your score. If you knew most of them, you're ready to make a fishing trip before the end of the week and you'll probably do really well. If you flunked miserably, though, go back and reread all the relevant chapters. And try not to use sharp objects!

Answers: 1—d, 2—b, 3—d, 4—b, 5—a, 6—b, 7—c, 8—a, 9—d, 10—a, 11—c, 12—d, 13—b, 14—b, 15—c, 16—b, 17—a, 18—c, 19—b, 20—b, 21—c, 22—a, 23—b, 24—d, 25—b.

CHAPTER 41

The Effects of Weather on Fishing

Regardless of where you pursue the sport, the weather and all of its elements greatly affect fishing, both recreational and commercial.

Winds, which generally cause extremely rough water in unprotected areas, keep fishermen from going out to make their catches. Winds also dirty the waters due to wave action, thereby decreasing the fish's ability to find bait.

Rain dilutes the salinity of the water, changing it from salt to brackish to fresh, sometimes in only hours. The change sometimes causes fish not to feed (and not to bite). Rain also washes off urban pollution—car exhaust, engine oil, fertilizers, mud, and Lord knows what all else—and dumps it directly into lakes, bayous, and streams, thereby dirtying the water even more (and sometimes biologically affecting the fish).

Temperature affects not only the fishermen but the fish as well. When it's cold, fishermen often get downright miserable out on the water—they get wet, they chill easily, and because of the temperatures they don't perform nearly as effectively as they would when it's warm and pleasant. But cold temperatures also greatly affect the fish—they become less aggressive, more sluggish, and sometimes not very hungry (which means that if they get too cold they just don't bite).

Pressure, as in barometric pressure, is a major factor in fishing success and failure. Of all the weather elements, this one is probably the biggest player. One normal unit of pressure is equivalent to one atmosphere of weight pressing down on us—this is what we feel every day. When the pressure decreases (as when a low-pressure system comes through and it turns stormy), the fish feel that and to them it signifies a change. When the pressure increases (as when a high-pressure system comes through and produces a "bluebird" day), the fish feel that too and to them it signifies a change. That's because the pressure on the surface of the water is felt equally on the bottom (where many of the fish hang out). Oh, and remember, the reason why this affects fishing is that *fish don't like change!*

CHAPTER 42

Fishing Trickery That Rookies Need to Know

There are a lot more things that rookie fishermen can do.

CHUMMING

You can *chum*. Yeah, I know, chumming is one of those really popular fishing tricks they use down in Costa Rica, or over in the Amazon, and even in the wide-open, deepwater Gulf of Mexico. But did you know that you could chum in all of the places *we* fish? Let me explain: chum is nothing more than bits of ground-up fish or shrimp that you cast overboard as a semisolid liquid to attract game fish to the "smell." And I gotta tell you it does make a difference in whether you catch fish or you don't!

Think of it as walking into a kitchen and having the aroma of a succulently roasted chicken smack you in the nostrils. Immediately you're starving, right? Well, the principle works the same for fish. And since some fish can even smell in "parts per million," chum is a really good way to make them ravenous. Just be sure your chum is so finely ground it doesn't come off as a "snack." You don't want to feed the fish; you just want to whet their appetites.

The effectiveness of this "trickery" was proven back when I was on the staff of the Louisiana Wildlife and Fisheries Department. At the time I worked with a really great marine biologist named David John. He told me he was having trouble collecting fish for his studies, so I showed him a little invention I had come up with—the chumsicle. He made one, used it, attracted more fish than he ever thought existed, and eventually relied on chumsicles for years to do his research. Here's how you construct them.

Take a regular half-gallon waxed milk carton, rinse it out well, and completely unfold and open the top end. Then take a regular wire clothes hanger, grab the hook end in one hand and the center of the horizontal crossbar that forms the base of the hanger in the other hand, and pull them in opposite directions until you completely elongate the wire. (Keep the hook intact, though.)

Then fold over the elongated portion into thirds and insert the folds into the milk carton, leaving the hook end out of the carton and fully exposed. If you've done it right, the triple fold should fit very snugly against the inside walls of the milk carton, forming the framing that will hold the frozen concoction together.

Now, using only enough water to make the mixture soupy, grind up fish carcasses and shrimp heads in a blender and pour the "soup" into the milk carton. Then fold the flaps of the milk carton closed again and staple them together (once more, the hook is outside the closure). At this point all you do is freeze the "sicle" solid.

Then when you're ready to fish, take the carton from the freezer, drape it over the gunwale of the boat with the hook end of the hanger, and stab enough holes in the carton to allow the mixture to leak out as it slowly defrosts. Melted chum dripping into the water forms an irresistible slick, which is guaranteed to attract every fish within blocks to your boat and put them into a frenzy to feed. Neat trick, huh? And it works!

ZONE LEVELS

Of course, you can drop over chumsicles by the six-pack and attract every fish in the northern gulf to your boat, but if you don't fish the proper *zone* level you're still not going to catch anything. To nail fish consistently you first have to find their feeding zone.

They might be close to the surface, in which case you'll either have to cast and rip the bait across the water to keep it riding up high in the water column, or suspend the bait under a float of some sort (either the rattling or chugging type).

They may be at midlevel, in which case you first need to cast then retrieve the bait slower than usual, to allow it to sink to a middepth range. This is probably the most difficult ranging tactic to master since it is regulated solely by retrieval speed. Don't be discouraged if it takes you a little while to do this effectively.

And finally, *they may be feeding close to the bottom,* in which case you need to cast, allow time for the bait to settle to the bottom, and then begin a bouncing, twitching, erratic retrieve that will entice bottom-feeding fish to inhale the nose-bumping, grubbing bait.

But wait! Okay—I sense the question you're pondering. How do you know when to use which of these zone tactics? What magic is there in the ether that tells you whether to fish shallow or midrange or deep? The answer is . . . *you don't and there isn't any!* You simply have to try them all, every time you select a new spot to fish. It's what the pros do. And it's the secret to how those TV fishing guys catch fish all the time (no, we really don't have divers under the boat hookin' on trout we buy at the New Orleans Fish House!).

Here's the applied technique:

The first thing you do is pull up to a location (and remember what you read in this book about being superquiet!). Then you begin *fancasting* to evaluate the area. You fancast by standing in one spot on the boat and laying down a pattern of casts one after the other that resembles a hand-fan, zero to 180 degrees in an arc, testing the water at each angle for a strike.

What's more, to do it right you should not only fancast but *fancast at every zone*—surface, midrange, and bottom. All too often, fish are stacked up at only one particular point in the "fan" and one particular zone level. Too many fishermen have made the mistake of pulling up to an area, halfheartedly casting twice off the starboard bow, say, then weighing anchor and heading off to another spot. If only they had made several casts about 20 degrees to the left and gone down a little deeper in the zone, they would have found limits of fish suspending over the shell bank! But you never thought it was that critical, did you?

MATCH THE HATCH

Up North, my Yankee friends have an expression. They say, "Match the hatch." What it means is that you should always, always endeavor to fish with whatever appears to be dominant in the water table. Do that and you will also catch fish consistently.

For example, if you see glass minnows popping on the surface everywhere you look, to scientifically maximize your chance of catching whatever sport fish occupies the area, you should fish either with real glass minnows or something in your tackle box that closely resembles them. If shrimp are popping everywhere, fish either with real shrimp or some artificial lure that resembles shrimp.

But let's say you don't see the bait in the water. How do you match the hatch then? Simple—once you catch that first fish, whip out the ol' fillet knife, remove the fish's stomach, and see what the critter you just caught has selected as his favorite main dish du jour. Then you fish with that or something in your tackle box that closely resembles that! It works every time.

Of course, it's time that I share with you a little bit of *natural vs. artificial* "trickery." A damn good fisherman will have live, market, and artificial bait with him on every trip, because sometimes fish want nothing but live. Sometimes they won't touch live but will tear up only the hard and soft plastics. Sometimes you'll need live bait to get them started—*or maybe even to find them to begin with*—and then you can switch over to artificials to save on the cost of natural bait and speed up the fish-catching process.

But wait a minute! Is the real issue "bait that's real or artificial"? Not at all—it's learning how to make that item with which you are fishing appear appetizing and irresistibly edible to the fish you want to eat it!

CHAPTER 43

And Even More Tricks for Trout

So okay . . . you've gleaned the trays and scoured the drawers and you're convinced that you now have only the proven essentials in your tackle box. What's more, you're confident that you're also armed with only the most productive and sophisticated rods and reels, rigged the way they're supposed to be rigged for catching speckled trout. So whaddaya do now? Well, now you learn about the hardest part. Now you gotta learn all the tricks!

TRICKS FOR LIVE BAIT

Trout prefer three kinds—shrimp, Cocahoe minnows, and baby croakers. Shrimp are the most productive bait all across Southeastern Louisiana from about May through mid-July, then again from late August until late December. Why should be obvious—it's the peak of the shrimp season, when both brown and white shrimp take up residence along the coast.

I recommend that whenever possible (that means when the tidal range is about six-tenths of a foot or less, since a "hard tide" won't allow the bait to work effectively) you fish live shrimp by rigging them weightless (no sinker, no split-shot, no nothing!) on a Kahle hook and fish them freeline in the current. And if you want to increase the frequency of the strikes, run the hook through the second-to-last segment near the tail (you won't hit a vital organ that way and the shrimp will stay alive longer). It's a sensitive style of fishing, but you'll know he's there when he picks up the bait and straightens out the line.

Cocahoes are productive almost anytime, but they seem to attract more attention during the cooler months. They, too, should be fished on a 2/0 or 3/0 Kahle hook, either freeline or down on the bottom behind a sliding sinker on a Carolina rig. If you notice, however, that the trout appear to be striking surface baits, a Cocahoe dangled on an 18-inch shock leader under a rattling cork makes for a dynamite arrangement.

Of course, some anglers just remove the plastic tail from a quarter-ounce leadhead jig (actually three-eighths ounce is more productive if you fish in Lake Pontchartrain) and attach a live Cocahoe to the hook. While this tactic will catch some fish (when they're really thick), it's just not the scientific way to do it! And by the way, Cocahoes should always be hooked through the lips. Oh, yeah—and they should not only be *live;* they should be *lively!*

Real trout masters, though, prefer to fish baby croakers whenever they are available. These little baitfish are killers when it comes to catching big trout. If you are fishing under a cork, they are best hooked through the meaty "shoulder" portion just before the forward dorsal fin. To my way of thinking, they should only be fished freeline, whenever practical (hook tied directly to monofilament without any sort of weight whatsoever), but if freelining is not possible, a Carolina rig will usually get you some action. In the case of the freeline or Carolina rig, hook the croaker through the lips.

Trout seem not to bite as rapidly on croakers, but when they do, you can make book that they're the hawgs! The only other bait that will take bigger fish than baby croakers are live pogeys—see chapter 25 about those.

TRICKS FOR TERMINAL RIGGINGS

Regardless of what anyone says, there's no one hard and fast way to fish either natural or artificial bait for speckled trout. It all depends on where you're fishing, what the conditions are, what the pattern is, the time of year, and so forth. But I can guarantee you that one of the following techniques will work at any given time.

1. Use a plastic tail on a jig head, tied directly to the monofilament or braided line, for cast and retrieve. To initiate a strike, you may have to bounce it off the bottom, vary the retrieve, rip it across the water, or just twitch it intermittently. The secret, though, is not to use too heavy a jig head or too heavy a line. Quarter-ounce lead is considered by the pros to be the standard for jigs; PowerPro braided line (8/30) is the choice of most veteran fishermen. I give you these suggested specifics because over the years I've found that fishermen always tend to fish too heavy!

2. Use a live Cocahoe on a jig head tied directly to the monofilament or braided line for bottom-fishing. It's not the right way to do it, but if it works, hey, who can argue with a proven approach?

3. Rig a sliding sinker above a barrel swivel, tied to a 12- to 14-inch shock leader, which is then tied directly to a Kahle hook baited with a live Cocahoe or croaker for bottom-fishing. This is the famed "Carolina," best used in a stronger current when freelining won't allow you to get the bait down to where the fish are feeding.

4. Tie the monofilament or braided line directly to a rattling or popping cork, which is tied to a shock leader, which is tied to a Kahle hook, which is baited either with a live shrimp, live Cocahoe, or live croaker for float fishing. Over the years I've discovered that the depth of the leader needs to be varied depending upon the feeding level of the fish. And depending upon the liveliness of the bait, you might want to add a split-shot to the leader to keep the little rascal in the strike zone.

5. Tie the monofilament or braided line directly to a rattling or popping cork, which is tied to a shock leader, which is tied to a quarter-ounce jig head, which is fitted with a split-tail beetle for float fishing. You can experiment if you want to, but for my money, absolutely no color in the rainbow beats a chartreuse with a red hotspot! There's something about the li'l critter!

6. And finally, tie the monofilament or braided line directly to a topwater lure for surface fishing. This is the ideal technique to use when you're out on those slick summer mornings right at daybreak when the trout are feeding on the top. To watch a monster speck explode on a floating plug can stop your heart!

TRICKS ABOUT WHERE TO FISH

Believe it or not, there is a scientific list of prime spots.

Centerline channels—they're the "swinging doors" of the marine cafeteria. This is where the tidal flow moves bait into and out of an estuary. It's where trout, and many other species, congregate to feed.

Shoreline reefs and sandbars—if the channels are the swinging doors, then these are the main dining rooms. Lots of bait collect at these places, and where you find little fish, you find big fish that want to eat 'em!

Junctions of canals with bays or lagoons—another prime baitfish-funneling area. These are usually eroded-bottom spots, where the rise and fall of the tide has deepened the water and provided a "false refuge" for all the baitfish in the area. They tend to congregate here, so predatory fish congregate here too.

Outfalls and trainaisses—these are especially productive when falling tides suction water out of the marsh into the primary waterway. Predatory species instinctively wait at these "funnels" with jaws agape to snatch up whatever comes down the pike under the influence of the current.

Open bays—the ideal spots in summer, though mostly for school-size fish when trout are traveling in schools. You can tell when these places are hot and producing—you'll see the seagulls diving right where the schools are suspended. Fish the birds and you'll find the fish.

Shallow flats—again, this is one of those standard schooling areas for trout, but sometimes the more hefty of the species are part of the mix. The flats, especially those comprised mostly of oyster reefs, is one of those places you should never pass up.

AND THE REST IS GOSPEL!

If you've always asked, "Why can my brother-in-law, or my neighbor down the street, or my buddy at work catch fish every time they go?" the answer is simple. They follow the "Alpha Fishing Gospel."

Ever since day one, man (and yes, perhaps woman—Eve probably wet a line every now and then) has been by trial and error determining what does and doesn't catch fish. So after all this time, the methodology has been inscribed in stone. The seriously enlightened hold such Scripture dear to their hearts (and they usually catch fish!). So if you'd like to join the ranks of the piscatorial apostles, here's the gospel . . . chapter and verse:

1. Study all your maps and charts prior to going fishing. You've got to know where you're going and where the fish probably will be.

2. Find the cleanest, clearest water available. Fish breathe the stuff—they won't hang around where it will clog up their gills, or where it won't allow them to spot a possible meal. Be cautious, though. Sometimes it's dirty on the surface but nice and clean underneath. If you watch your wheelwash, it's easy to tell.

3. Always fish a moving tide! True, most coastal fishing is best on a falling tide, but it really makes no difference if it's incoming or outgoing, so long as it's moving. Think of an estuary as a cafeteria—when the doors are closed you can't get to the food. Open the doors and it's time to eat. Moving tide moves bait!

4. Fish "with the tide" rather than against it for a more natural approach. Let's say the tide is moving to the east, and all the bait is moving to the east. But along you come pulling one single baitfish to the west. If you were a trout, would you believe that?

5. Use a trolling motor or drift-fish. The days are gone when you could anchor in one spot and wait for the fish to come to you. You want to catch fish? You've got to go find them! Anchor only when you find them stacked up.

6. Look for baitfish action on the water. This should be obvious, but I've seen so many fishermen pass up spots that

were dead giveaways to feeding trout. And always stop to fish under a school of mullets! Just about everything feeds on the poor mullet. Who knows? There could be a big school of big specks swimming right under them!

7. Vary your cast and retrieve from "ripping" to "dead slow." Trout feed with different intensities every day (sometimes every hour). It isn't uncommon to start catching fish just by changing the way you're fishing.

8. Learn to "twitch" rather than "jerk and snap." I honestly believe that the tactics have changed over the decades. When I was a kid fishing for trout, we always jerked the spots off the lure just to give it some action. But keep in mind that in those days we were fishing with shad rigs and hard plastics. Today, most trout are caught with a subtler, gentler "twitch" than a "jerk," where you use only the rod tip and wrist action to move the lure. This is best achieved if your elbow is kept locked at your side.

9. Learn to "chug" a cork and when to reel it in. Again, just the wrist action is enough to create a popping sound on the water, which in turn will get a fish's attention. But here's the gospel—after the bait strikes the water, if a fish is anywhere in the area he'll strike at it within four or five good chugs. I mean, it's irresistible! If you get no takers in that period of time, reel it in and cast in another spot.

10. Rig your plastic beetles and Cocahoes to run *true* (not all cockeyed). Insert the hook into the plastic on a straight line, not tilted off to one side or the other, or bunched up in an arch. Also avoid using artificials in tandem. I know, the old-timers just love the possibility of "ketchin' dem doubles!" but it's much easier to feel the subtle sensitivities of a strike with only one bait tied to the line, especially if the line is braided.

11. And the most important words of the gospel, "No Fish in 15—Move!" You've seen this elsewhere in this book. But I ask you again, if you've been sitting in one spot for 15 minutes and you ain't even had a bite, why would you stay there?

So at this point, you probably think you know more about speckled trout than you ever wanted to. But guess what?

CHAPTER 44

Trout-Catchin' Tactics 101

Just call me the professor! Because between my television shows, personal appearances, professional seminars, chats in the mall, and conversations at the boat launch, I probably spend the greater part of my time discussing with fellow fishermen the tactics and techniques of catching more fish—primarily speckled trout. So I figured, why not take the opportunity afforded by this chapter to teach a nitty-gritty, down-and-dirty, cum-laude, "how-to" lesson on catching trout?

In the precisely organized lesson plan that follows, I'll strip away the sugar coatings, separate the wheat from the chaff, and chip off all of the gingerbread to get to the plain vanilla manna from heaven (you can call them tricks if you want to) for increasing your success when it comes to finding and limiting out on trout.

So here it is—all the technology you need to know, explained in detail and easy to understand. Read it, study it, make yourself a copy of it, and put it in your tackle box for future reference. But most importantly, put it to practice.

WHAT SHOULD BE IN YOUR TACKLE BOX

Most of us don't carry tackle boxes; we carry sporting-goods stores! Believe me, about 90 percent of what we take along on a fishing trip could be left at home (or better yet, thrown away!). A small knife, a pair of scissors, a set of wire cutters, a pair of pointy-nose pliers, a fish grabber, a can of lube, a bottle of insect spray, and a tube of suntan lotion should be the extent of what we label the "accessories." But if you really want to deep-six the extraneous junk, you've got to get rid of the so-called "tackle," all those hooks and baits and plugs and lures you bought that were guaranteed to work but don't.

Basically, here's what you need—and all you need!—to consistently catch speckled trout:

1. *An assortment of jig heads*—but you don't need them in every color of the rainbow. Of course, the tackle salesman at Super-Mart told you that you did, so you took his word for it and bought the entire spectrum. But the truth of the matter is you can stash in the trays of your tackle box about *a dozen, round-head, unpainted, lead jigs* and catch just as many trout as the next guy—and maybe more. The oval-shaped, teardrop-shaped, bullet-shaped, and pony-shaped heads are all jig heads designed by the manufacturer to get you to buy more tackle, not catch more fish. Your assortment should include jig heads by weight—$1/4$ ounce, $3/8$ ounce, $1/2$ ounce, and $3/4$ ounce. It's the weight that gets the lure to the feeding level, not the shape and color of the head.

2. *An assortment of plastic tails*—but again, you really only need a handful of colors to catch any trout that swims. Most of us have invested hundreds of dollars in plastic tails, gradually amassing them on the recommendations of our fishing buddies. You remember, don't you, how Harry told us that this one pinky-purple color caught fish last Friday at Delacroix Island, which immediately prompted us to rush out and buy 250 copies of that pinky-purple color so that we wouldn't run out? Well, after about a year of collecting all those "certain" colors (which we hardly ever use), we need a forklift to pick up our tackle boxes to put them into the boat. And the sad part of it all is that very few of those "buddy-recommended colors" ever caught anything!

Let me tell you what you really need. When it comes to plastic tails and catching trout, you should have in your tackle box about a dozen each of Cocahoe minnow tails, split-tail beetles, and grub tails. The Cocahoes are most effective whenever shrimp season is closed, because at those times most of the shrimp are offshore, which means inshore trout feed primarily on live minnows. The beetles and grub tails are most effective during shrimp season, because at those times trout feed primarily on shrimp. Of course, this isn't iron-clad science—there are times when trout will take Cocahoes, beetles, and grubs all in the same day at the same place.

For that reason, the "action" you give to a lure is the key to how it produces. Because Cocahoe tails are designed by their manufacturers to be swimming baits, they provide their own action as a lure. Beetles and grubs, however, need to be "worked" by the fisherman to give those lures their action. The bottom line, though, is that any artificial bait must be made to appear enticing and edible to a fish. So when either bait is fished properly, regardless of the time of year, trout will strike it aggressively.

But what about color? While plastic baits are molded and shot in over 300 different color combinations, virtually every veteran fisherman will tell you that all you need to use are 10 common colors to catch trout consistently. They are white, iridescent (glow in the dark), pearl, tuxedo (pearl body with a black back), sparkled chartreuse, avocado, strawberry, motor oil, smoke flake, and purple with a chartreuse tail. All the other colors you see hanging on the walls at the sporting-goods stores (or taking up space in your tackle box), in spite of how the brochures read or what the salesman told you, were designed to catch fishermen, not fish.

The white, glow in the dark, pearl, and tuxedo are best used on bright days when water clarity is good. The sparkled chartreuse, avocado, and strawberry work best on partly cloudy days in moderate water clarity. And the motor oil, smoke flake, and purple are most effective on overcast dark days. It really makes no difference where you fish—Delacroix, Golden Meadow, Lafitte, Venice, and everyplace in between—these colors produce strikes. But it's important to remember that whether you use Cocahoe tails, beetles, or grubs in these colors, the tails should be threaded on the hook as straight as possible so that the baits run true and provide "natural" action.

The only other artificial lures you need in your tackle box to catch trout are commonly referred to as "topwaters"—floating stick baits designed to cause fish to strike on the surface. Of the many hundreds on the market, the most common (and most productive) in Louisiana waters are the Mirror-Lures in red and silver, blue and silver, green and silver, and solid gold; the Zara Spooks in red and silver, blue and silver, black and white, and solid black; and the Rapalas in black and silver, black and gold, and the broken-backs. Oh, yeah—and the "Top Dog," the new kid on the block, is starting to make a few waves, too.

At this point your tackle box should be starting to shape up. The only other things that I see you needing are

1. *Small barrel swivels*—use them to make sliding sinker rigs (the so-called Carolina rigs) and for live-bait fishing with a shock leader under a rattling cork. Oh, for the record, do not ever use *snap swivels* to attach lead jig heads to your monofilament for artificial-bait fishing—snap swivels change the action of the lure.

2. *Rattling corks*—use them above a 14-inch shock leader to float a bait just under the surface when trout are feeding off the bottom. Rattling corks have recently become the float of choice over the old popping corks because they don't become as tangled in the line as popping corks do, and because the noise they make is believed to attract more fish.

3. *20- or 30-pound shock leader material*—use it to make leaders for sliding sinker rigs and for shock leaders under a rattling cork. I recommend these pound-test weights for both artificial- and live-bait fishing.

4. *Split-shot* (assorted weights up to a quarter ounce)— depending upon the pull of the current, attach them to the shock leader about halfway between the rattling cork and the Kahle hook to sink a live bait below the surface. You don't need them if you're fishing plastic baits on a jig head.

5. *Rubber-core, crimp, and sliding egg sinkers*—use rubber-core and crimp sinkers to add weight to terminal rigging when fishing live or market bait (dead shrimp, cracked crab, etc.). Use the egg sinker to make a sliding sinker rig. First thread the monofilament coming through the rod guides through the sinker. Then tie on a barrel swivel to act as a stop for the sinker. Then attach whatever length leader (usually two feet) to the opposite end of the barrel swivel and rig a Kahle hook at the terminal end.

6. *2/0, 3/0, and 4/0 Kahle hooks*—if you're still using old-style conventional fish hooks, toss 'em out! The Kahle hook has taken over as the primo hook, especially for speckled-trout fishing. Its unusual curvature produces a greater hook-set and results in fewer hooks being "spit," especially by bigger trout. I suggest you have all three of these sizes in your tackle box.

Up to this point, we've focused specifically on what should be in a good trout fisherman's tackle box. So now it's time to highlight the armaments necessary for putting those trout in the boat, namely rods, reels, and line.

BAITCASTING VS. SPINNING

That's been the primary question ever since Izaak Walton bought his first minnow bucket. Of course, the bottom-line answer is, "Since you have to fish with it, fish with what you like." If you've mastered a baitcasting rig to the extent of minimizing your backlashes (rats' nests), then fish exclusively with baitcasting. If, on the other hand, you prefer the hassle-free features of a spinning rig, then fish spinning. Don't feel as if the tackle type is a prestige thing—it's not! Both baitcasting and spinning rigs will catch fish. And besides, nowhere does it say that if you don't use the same kind of tackle you see the "pros" use on the ESPN fishing shows on Saturday mornings, you'll never be a real fisherman.

But if you want the ultimate answer, I believe that a good fisherman (any kind of fisherman!) should take both kinds of rigs on every trip out: baitcasting for those ideal windless days and spinning for those blustery days when you have to cast into the wind (it's a pain throwing baitcasting tackle into the wind!).

More important than what kind of rig you fish with is the *quality* of the rig you fish with. The blister-pak rod and reel combos, the sale clearance specials at the corner bait shop, and the three-dollar complete fishin'-pole steal at the garage sale down the block are the world's worst bargains!

First, they'll probably work for all of about 15 minutes before they fall apart on the first decent strike (if you ever feel the strike). And they'll no doubt cast like a telephone pole and feel about as heavy at the end of the day. Here's your rule of thumb—it's better to have only *one* good rod and reel than *five* pitiful ones.

For that reason, I suggest that you never ever buy a combo set that someone at the big-department-store, sporting-goods counter already put together for you. I mean, does it make sense to you that the little high-school-sophomore girl working part-time on weekends at the Stuf-Mart is qualified to match and balance rods to reels for serious fishermen? So why, then, would you plop down your hard-earned cash for a rig like that?

Did you notice I said *match and balance?* A good rod-and-reel rig *has to be* matched and balanced, whether you're catching trout or triggerfish. That means you buy the rod and reel as separate units but at the same time, so that one fits the other like a glove. In other words, don't buy a reel, take it home, stash it in a drawer, then go back two weeks later (with the reel still at home in the drawer) and buy a rod to fit it. The two will never match in action, function, or weight. And only by the grace of God will they balance without being top-heavy on one end or the other.

Which brings up another good point, especially for trout fishing. Avoid choosing tackle that's too heavy to feel the strikes. My old friend and personal Golden Meadow fishing guide, John Aucoin, will tell you that there are times during the year when big mule trout—five pounds and upward—will barely mouth the bait. No locomotive attacks. No vicious assaults. Sometimes not even a solid "bump." So can you imagine how many of these fish you'll never catch (and never feel on the line) because you were fishing with a broomstick?

Trust me, a good medium-weight, graphite, brand-name rod with enough backbone to set the hook is all you need to catch your share of speckled trout. You want it to have flexibility in the tip, but just in the tip. If it's too springy, between it and the monofilament stretch you'll never get a good hookset. On the other hand, if it's too stiff, every time you set the hook you'll rip it out of the fish's mouth. A suitable price range is somewhere between $40 and $60.

Of course, the rod isn't worth a plug nickel if you have a trashy reel seated on it. Never never buy a bargain reel! Remember the old expression "you get what you pay for"? Well, it was never more true than for fishing reels. Generally, you can expect to pay at least $65 for a quality reel. And whether you choose baitcast or spinning, it should be velvety smooth when cranked and house at least three ball bearings (preferably five). Oh—and a good overall gear ratio (especially for big speckled trout) is five to one.

Now up to this point, we've been talking about using one rod and reel only. Ideally, though, the ultimate trout-fishing tactic is to have several rods and reels pre-rigged in a variety of different configurations. After all, you'll never know where the trout will be on any given day, what feeding pattern they'll be on, and what baits they will and will not take. If you're using only one rod and reel, you'll constantly have to cut and retie the line to change terminal tackle—a Cocahoe tail, a sliding sinker, a freeline hook, a topwater plug, and a rattling cork all mean interruptions of your fishing time. With several rods and reels pre-rigged specifically for rattling-cork fishing, cast and retrieve, topwater chugging, and bottom bouncing, you never stop fishing once!

THE SCOOP ON LINE

The only other armament equally as important as the quality

of the rod and reel is the line you have on the reel. Ever since I was a kid just learning to fish, the mindset has been "use a strong enough line to keep the fish from breaking it and getting away." Of course, those were the days of old braided Dacron, when legitimate fishermen used 50-pound-test line to land half-pound croakers. All I can say is thank the Good Lord that fishing attitudes and technology have changed—and improved!

We now know that you get more strikes you can feel, have more fun fishing, become more of a sportsman, and land as many if not more fish using light monofilament—say, 12- and 15-pound test—as opposed to using anchor rope.

But again, the name of the tune is "quality." Cheap, bargain-basement line never has produced and never will produce good fishermen (to say nothing of good fishing). If you want the ultimate, if you want to do it right, invest in only premium monofilament. My personal choice is Berkley Trilene Big Game, not because they're a sponsor (they aren't), not because I get free line (I don't), and not because it's cheap (it isn't), but because in spite of my having abused it way past its tolerances, it has still stood up to some of the most rigorous wear and tear without ever failing when it counted. Of course, there are other high-performance, premium brands on the market you may choose from, provided you follow a couple of commandments:

1. Be sure you always properly set the reel drag to reduce the possibility of line breakage. Yes, Virginia, you can catch a 100-pound tuna on 10-pound-test line if you set the drag right. You don't need to use wire rope!

2. Always, always, always retie the terminal tackle whenever you feel it's necessary after catching several big fish. During the time of year when the mule trout are in, I suggest you routinely snip off about 36 inches of monofilament and retie your bait, say, after every six fish. You might be thinking that's excessive, but big trout (and especially big reds!) can cause serious abrasions to monofilament. I, for one, don't want to

take any chances of losing a record fish just because I didn't take time to cut off the frayed line and retie the bait.

As far as color is concerned, most veteran trout fishermen will attest that it's purely a matter of personal preference. You can use the clear or the green tint. Guys who regularly catch fish do so on both.

More important than color is the pound test. I suggest that for optimum speckled-trout fishing across coastal Louisiana, you run the spectrum anywhere from 12- to 20-pound test, depending upon the reel you use. Remember how I told you earlier about strike sensitivity—how sometimes a trout will just mouth the lure gently? Well, monofilament line this light will give you the subtlety it takes to feel the bite. Anything heavier is overkill and counterproductive!

And finally, should you use regular old monofilament or opt for the new state-of-the-art braided line? Let's put it this way—braided line provides the ultimate in sensitivity. But you've got to learn how to fish it properly. It is entirely different from mono and absolutely cannot be fished like it.

I prefer the PowerPro brand, but I suggest you try various others and choose your own personal favorite. And while I do sometimes use the 8/30 (8-pound-test diameter equivalence with a breaking strength approaching 30-pound test) on my baitcasting reels, I always use the 8/30 braided line on my spinning reels. I just like the way it performs!

For casting under bridge pilings, for twitching and jerking over clusters of oyster reefs, for trolling the trestle, for jigging sheepshead up off the bottom of a canal, or for turning a bull red away from the base of an oil rig, *braided* is *primo* stuff!

CHAPTER 45

Litany of the Lake

All the veteran fishmasters will brazenly confirm that there is unquestionably a protocol, a set of commandments if you will, that absolutely must be followed to the letter if you intend to consistently pull trout out from under the bridges in Lake Pontchartrain. Opt not to follow these commandments and you'll forever return to the docks with practically nothing to show for your daylong efforts on the water. This chapter, therefore, is designed to lay out the fishing Scripture so that as soon as you finish reading it, you can head out to "the bridges" and bring home a trout dinner. Can I have an "amen"?

Get up early in the morning so that you can fish the traditional prime daybreak period—it's the time when most fishermen head out on the water.

Or check the tide charts carefully for the I-10 Twin Spans and plan to be on the water to catch optimum tidal movement—this is when the fish bite best every day.

Have your boat loaded with drinks (especially lots of bottled water), a sandwich or two, all your USCG-required safety equipment, an extra deep-cycle battery, and a fully charged cell phone. Also make sure you bring aboard at least three rods and reels—one rigged Carolina style, one rigged with a 3/8-ounce, plain, round, unpainted jig head, and one rigged with a Rat-L-Trap for trolling.

Launch out of Tite's Place at the foot of the Five-Mile

Bridge on Highway 11 at North Shore in time to be on the water *before the sun comes up*. The later you get on the water, the more of the morning fishing action you're going to miss (unless, of course, peak tide is later in the day). It is not uncommon, and it never has been, for most of the bites to take place during the first hour or two after sunup, then stop completely thereafter for the remainder of the day. In Lake Pontchartrain, there really is some basis for the old expression "you snooze, you lose!"

Turn on the live well and superstock it with both live shrimp and—if you can find them—live croakers. If you have a tendency to skimp on the amount of live bait you bring with you, remember that during trout season, when your live bait is gone, the fish stop biting. Period! That's because the lake every spring, summer, and fall is full of live shrimp—it's the principal component in a fish's diet. Except for live baby croakers, which are the "filet mignon of the trout menu"! So bring along croakers whenever you can get them.

Just as a safety blanket, you might want to stash a cast net aboard your boat until late fall, so that if you can't find live bait (and Tite's usually has all you want), you can make a few casts on the way out in an attempt to catch your own. Don't shrug off any option—cover all your bases.

Crank the outboard, head into the lake, go past the north drawbridge, and proceed directly to Railroad Marker 176 on the train trestle (which is almost at middle lake).

Drop both a bow and a stern anchor to position the boat parallel to the trestle about 30 yards off the pilings. The objective here is to avoid having the boat swing with the tide.

Until the sun comes up good, fish under the bridge pilings, using either a three-eighths-ounce leadhead jig or a Carolina rig fitted with a three-eighths-ounce egg sinker. Initially, expect to catch mostly flounder and sheepshead, but you could very easily get into the speckled trout, too. Just be certain you're fully on the bottom, which means you may have to adjust the size of the sinker to counteract tidal pull.

Count on the bites to be subtle—just a few rapid taps and then the sensation of weight on your line, almost as if you've hung a snag. When you feel the taps, do nothing. Just get ready. When you feel the "snag" weight, set the hook hard and hold on. The flounder or sheepshead will be there every time! If it's a trout that happens to pick up your live shrimp, sometimes there won't be a tap or the sensation of a snag—rather the fish will try to pull the rod completely out of your hand. Of course, if you do any of this wrong, you'll lose a bait every time!

Now once the sun comes up pretty good (say around nine o'clock or so), switch around and begin fishing *away* from the trestle, making long casts that stretch out about 20 yards off the gunwale of the boat. This is the time you begin fishing exclusively for big trout, and most of the ones you'll catch during prime season will exceed four pounds apiece (actually, two to five pounds is a good anticipated average).

Again, fish with a Carolina rig (about 16 inches long) and use a three-eighths-ounce sliding egg sinker. If you've got them, substitute live croakers for the live shrimp. Of course, if you can't find croakers at Tite's and you have no luck throwing the cast net for your own, stay with the live shrimp. But fish them directly on the bottom.

Actually, all you do is make the cast, allow the bait to sink all the way to the bottom, lock down the bail, and let it sit. Don't pop it, don't twitch it, don't jerk it, don't even move it. Just keep a tight line. When the trout spots the croaker, it will pick it up, take a moment or two to position it in its jaws, and swallow the baitfish headfirst. Contain your emotions while all this is going on! Don't try to set the hook! Just wait patiently! Because all of a sudden the fish is going to race away, fully bend your rod tip downward, and stretch your monofilament almost to the breaking point. When that happens, just pull against the force and the fish will hook itself! Don't do a "bass set." Don't try to cross its eyes! If you attempt that, or if you set the hook immediately upon feeling the taps at the terminal end, you will most certainly lose every trout that bites, because you will pull the bait right back out of its mouth. Oh, yeah—and never set the hook hard on big trout if you're using PowerPro or Spiderwire. Since both those products are made of braided line and there's no stretch in braided line, you'll lose the fish by pulling the hook free every time.

Be sure you set the drags on all your reels (baitcasting or spinning) before you make the first cast. If the drags are set too tight, these fish are going to pop lines! Also, don't horse them back to the boat. Be patient and play them properly. If they want to run, let them run. When they get tired, you'll be able to bring them right to the boat. Oh—and always use a landing net. Period! No exceptions!

Finally, and I know this is going to be a point of controversy, until midfall, if you insist on using artificials only, you may or may not catch any trout. Even the lake's veteran masters don't always do well only on artificials. Remember, you got to give them exactly what the want, and if it's live shrimp and baby croakers they want, then you'd best bring along some bait money!

What bridges produce fish consistently in Lake Pontchartrain? They all do—the trestle, the Highway 11 bridge, the I-10 Twin Spans, and, yes, even the Causeway.

The railroad trestle—start off fishing at Marker 176. Then try about a half-mile in either direction (first to the north side, then to the south side). You can crank up the big engine and move a block or two at a time, or you can just drop in the trolling motor and work your way along the pilings until you hit on some action. But the fish could be at any point along the trestle—you just have to find them. Usual hotspots, however, include 176, the Twin Signals, and the fenders south of the drawbridge. Oh, yeah—try fishing both the east and the west sides of the trestle. Depending upon the conditions, the fish may prefer one side over the other.

The Highway 11 bridge (Five-Mile)—start off fishing the south side about a half-mile off the shoreline. Then begin working your way toward the middle of the lake (again fishing both the east and west sides). "The Wedge" (the spot where the railroad trestle and the highway bridge come together near the North Draw) is another spot that traditionally holds fish. That should be your next choice. The highway bridge, however, is one of the primary "trolling" spots in the lake. So if you like to troll more than baitcast, start off fishing the highway bridge.

The I-10 Twin Spans—start off at the bridge fenders under the high-rise. Anchor on the west side of the bridge on the southern side of the fender, and cast to the fender. You will know right away if fish are holding there—they'll jump on your baits immediately if they are. If you get no action within five minutes, weigh anchor and head straight to the south side (I like to begin near the overhead sign that reads, "Irish Bayou/South Shore Next Exit").

You can fish the east side, the west side, or even between the two bridges. Always make your initial casts as close to the pilings as possible. If nothing happens, then begin fancasting, so that you cover all possible areas around your boat. You can try moving from spot to spot with the outboard, or you can test the full stretch of water along the bridge by using the trolling motor. Of course, when you hit on any kind of activity, ease the anchor over, work that one spot, and see what develops.

The Causeway—whether you launch on the north side at Mandeville or on the south side at Williams Boulevard or Bonnabel Boulevard, work these twin bridges out toward the middle of the lake. Crossovers are popular spots, and most Causeway fishermen put trout in the ice chest regularly by trolling. This bridge can be every bit as productive as the other three, but since it's 26 miles long, it usually takes longer to find the fish there.

If you don't have your own boat, rental boats and motors are available on a first-come first-serve basis at Tite's Place on Highway 11 at North Shore, and Capt. Kenny Kreeger regularly charters on Lake Pontchartrain (as do Dudley Vandeborre and Terry Googins).

So after having read all this, the only thing you really have to do next is get out on this 622-square-mile body of water and follow the litany of the lake!

CHAPTER 46

Those Good Ol' Fishin' Fables

I woke up out of a deep, sound sleep the night before last, sauntered down the hallway, and took my royal place on the porcelain throne in the hall bathroom. It seems that, like many other creative people I know, I do some profound thinking at that spot. So that's where, at around 20 minutes after two in the morning, I realized it's anybody's guess why some poor fishermen never catch anything at all. They've been given all the wrong rules, all the prefabricated mumbo-jumbo, all the bad leads, all the poor scoop, all the wrong poop, and way too much scientific gobbledygook. It's those little-known, rarely shared "fishing secrets" they really need to know. So in this chapter and verse, for the first time anywhere, I expose the errors in "Those Good Ol' Fishin' Fables" (all lies or exaggerations!).

Fable 1—to catch fish you must be on the water by sunup. That's because all fish like to have breakfast first thing in the morning. When that sun comes up, they're ready to eat. And they eat pretty quick, too! You wait 30, 40 minutes after sunup to get to the fishing spot and you may as well have gone to the mall with your mother-in-law! They're full by then. And scientifically, they probably couldn't eat another bite until sometime after noon or so. But that's another subject for another time.

Fable 2—the secret to make fish bite is to spit on your bait. This goes back to ancient times, before our ancestors invented toothbrushes and mouthwash and they had all manner of "aroma" just growing in their spit for days on end. Thus whenever they headed out to catch a mess of fish for the Saturday-night cave get-together, the natural fermentation in their spit acted as a modern-day attractant does and significantly increased their catches. Spitting on your bait really doesn't have the same effect in these modern times, but good fishermen still do it to preserve the age-old bond with our long-deceased elders.

Fable 3—you'll catch fish on every trip if you hold your mouth just right. This is a matter of semantics. Is it "to the right"? It can't be, because I've seen when "to the right" was "wrong." I truly believe that this particular fable could take up volumes, so I might address this in another book someday.

Fable 4—don't even think of fishing without removing all foreign scent from your hands before touching the lure. Now this is a major point of contention and has caused some heated confrontations at the marinas that operate bars! The general argument is that you gotta make sure you include all forms of "foreign scent." Gasoline, motor oil, bacon grease, jelly donuts, Preparation H, after-shave, Brill Creem—the list goes on and on! The guys in the lab at the Wildlife and Fisheries Department say fish can smell all these things, consider them to be "unnatural stinks," and consequently shun both artificial and live baits that smell anything like 'em. But if that's the case, how does one explain the next fable?

Fable 5—wanna catch lots of fish? Spray your bait with WD-40. Wait a minute! I don't remember any of the petrols and phenols you find in WD-40 as occurring in nature. And even though it's indisputable that fish spend a lot of time wet, I've never seen too many of them that have rusted. I could be wrong, but this sounds like one of those stories concocted by one of those guys who drives between Lafitte and Golden Meadow with sample cases of WD-40 spray cans stashed in the back of his '57 Buick station wagon, don't it?

Fable 6—fish never bite on a slack tide. The key word is "never." Anybody who has ever wet a line knows that at the exact minute that the tide stops, it's time to open a Chocolate

YooHoo, unwrap the Subway club with pickles and jalapenos, plug in your cell phone and order the Game Boy for your kid's birthday from QVC, slather another layer of zinc oxide on the bridge of your nose, or remove your shrimp boots and paint on some of that Fungi Nail your wife bought you for your tackle box. See, you've actually got time to do any or all of these things, because until you can spit in the water and see it drift away because the tide is once again moving, the only fish you'll catch will be certifiably suicidal!

Fable 7—fish always bite best on a falling tide. Didn't you just read Fable 6? Did it say anything about a rising or falling tide? It said a *moving* tide. Actually, both biologically and scientifically, it depends on where you're fishing and what you're fishing for as to whether fish bite best when the tide is rising or falling. But you can bet a bucket full of Cocahoe minnows that they'll all bite when the tide is moving and they'll all get lockjaw when it's not!

Fable 8—fish don't bite on a west wind. Fishermen argue over this all the time. And the truth is, some old-timers swear by this. Pro fishing guides, on the other hand, use this as an excuse when some of their "couldn't-catch-a-cold" charter fishermen turn up with three trout, two hardheads, and a needlefish after eight hours on the water. And, of course, most of your new-generation anglers totally dismiss this fable. The only time you really need to be concerned with it is if you don't even know which direction "west" is!

Fable 9—every fisherman knows you don't bring bananas on the boat. I'm not qualified to speak authoritatively on this subject. So you'll have to formulate your own beliefs here. I do know, however, that I've been thrown off a helluva lot of fishing boats when the people I was fishing with found out that I had stashed a banana in my lunch bag! Oh, yeah—and I can also tell you for a fact that you'll never get on *my* boat with a bunch of bananas! Superstitions are funny things, huh?

Fable 10—fishermen also know you don't bring hardboiled eggs on the boat. I'm not qualified to speak authoritatively on this subject either. So once again, draw your own conclusions. I do know, however, that I've been thrown off a helluva lot of fishing boats when the people I was fishing with found out that I had stashed a hardboiled-egg sandwich in my lunch bag! Oh, yeah—and I can also tell you for a fact that you'll never get on my boat with a hardboiled egg, even if we're fishing on Easter Sunday! Superstitions are funny things, huh?

Fable 11—never change to a fresh plastic bait until you absolutely have to, because the old bait will have the scent from the previous fish's mouth on it, which is an automatic attractant to other fish. But do you really suppose all trout are so easy-going they'll gladly allow their fellow trout to take a bite out of their plastic? I say that for the sake of hygiene, if you get a bite from, say, a drum and you miss the bite, change the lure right away. The next fish that hits certainly doesn't want drum slobber all over the lure he's about to dine on!

Fable 12—fish never bite when it's raining. You know, I heard this preached ever since I was a kid, but I'll be darned if I understand why. I mean, aren't fish already wet? So what can a little rain hurt? See, I personally believe that they bite better when it rains because the pounding of the raindrops forces fresh oxygen into the water . . . kinda like giving an old codger a shot of Viagra!

Fable 13—fish that jump don't bite. Betcha your grandpa used to tell you that, huh? And you probably went around telling people he was brilliant, too, didn't you? Actually, what Gramps was really saying to you was "fish don't bite while they're in the act of jumping," which really isn't all that difficult to comprehend if you think about it a little. How can a fish bite if he's in midair and the bait is in the water? Aw, never mind—let's just go to the next one.

Fable 14—the old-timers swear that anise oil is a good fish attractant. Actually, if you "set a spell" with some of dem old-timers on a park bench or under a pavilion at a boat launch, you'll find out pretty quick that old-timers have some pretty weird philosophies, not only about fish attractants but about practically everything. My experience has been that most of them can't remember to take their Metamucil every day, so how on Earth are they expected to remember that a flavoring that goes into Italian seed cookies will make a good fish attractant?

Fable 15—some fishermen say that garlic is the best fish attractant. I know Italian fishermen would be the first to tell you that, but I'm also certain that the Italians I know aren't about to waste their precious roasted garlic on the likes of channel mullet, gaspergou, gafftops, redfish, and even slimy ol' speckled trout. I suggest that fishermen who believe this garlic fable thing spend a little more time hanging out with some old-timers in the barbershop!

Fable 16—you won't catch any more trout once the dolphins move into an area. It all depends on just how menacing the dolphins look to the schools of speckled trout. If you got some real bold specks taking up residence over an oyster reef and they really dig the neighborhood, you can bet they're not going anywhere! But it's like everywhere you go—wimpy ol' trout will probably be bullied by a pod of 400-pound dolphins and haul it with their tails between their, uh, whatever!

Fable 17—you can't catch fish in dirty water. That's what you call a true generalization. Unfortunately, it's not true! Some fish, like croakers and gafftops and even redfish, actually love dirty water because they feed primarily by smell, not sight, and the murky water allows them to sneak up on their lunch. Trout, though, do bite best when the water is clean and clear. I think the real consideration here, though, should be "can you tell me what I.Q. some fishermen have who fish in the filthy drainage canals?" I mean, I've seen them on a Sunday morning pulling bluegills out from under the outflow culverts on the banks of the pesticide plant! And those fish go in the Igloo, too. Whoa!

Fable 18—there can be a time when the water can be too clear. All right, I'll give you that one. It has been my experience that when water is crystalline, especially along the bank when it's also exceptionally shallow, fish can see you coming and they will spook. Louisiana Wildlife and Fisheries folks *say a slightly opaque water column provides even odds for both the fisherman and the fish.* Of course, maybe the Wildlife and Fisheries people you know say that; the ones I know just say, "Can I see your license and your life jackets, please?"

Fable 19—you never ever catch fish you see. Wow—this is one profound statement, ain't it? *You never ever catch fish you see?* I've heard that applied to rolling tarpon, bedding bass, reds cruising the banks, and other species that you can "sight-fish." I guess this is one of those "brother-in-law axioms." Sometime way back in the early 1950s, brud-n-law probably heard one of the veteran Lake Pontchartrain tarpon fishermen at Lincoln Beach say, "You'll never catch the tarpon you see on the surface—it's that one down under him that'll take the bait!" Of course, being the rocket-scientist brud-n-law he is, he figured if that's the way it is for tarpon, that must be the way it is for every fish you see. Geeez! I don't guess we ought to tell him what the procedure is for spearfishing, huh?

Fable 20—10 percent of the fishermen catch 90 percent of the fish. I certainly believe that statement! And if you actually watch the way some people fish, you'll be tempted to raise the trailing percentage to about 96. But listen, I've decided not to comment anymore on this fable because I can remember the words of my Scoutmaster, who always told me, "Betta watch whatcha say, boy!"

Fable 21—fish never bite right after a full moon. It's because fish feed all night long *during* the full moon, so what kind of gluttonous fish would eat all night long and keep right on eating throughout the next day too? You want to be a really good fisherman? Always fish at night!

Fable 22—any crabs that you catch on a full moon will be really, really fat. I guess so—like fish, they eat all night during a full moon, too! Of course, I can't really prove this biologically, because I've never researched what exceptionally high-caloric nutrients night-feeding crabs really eat. Nevertheless, I'd wager a couple of good ham-and-cheese po' boys from

Shorty's in Meraux that, come the morning after a full moon, most crabs will tell you they're pretty stuffed (no pun intended)!

Fable 23—the shrimp that you catch when the moon is full will be really hard to peel. Bull-honkey! This statement is probably the most contrived one of all. Shrimp become hard to peel when you overcook them. How does this stuff get started?

Fable 24—when the tide is exceptionally high, redfish, sheepshead, and drum swim over the flooded land portions to eat snails. Yep—they eat snails, all right, and they also cruise this newfound virgin territory to eat baby crabs, fiddlers, clams, oysters, conchs, all kinds of minnows, baby ducks, newly hatched wading birds, tiny furbearers, discarded sandwiches, Moon Pies, and Firestone tires that brud-in-law dumped. I guess soon they'll eat out the whole marsh!

Fable 25—if you tie a balloon on the first trout you catch in the morning and immediately put him back in the water, he'll go right back to the school he came from and you can follow him all day. And as Forrest Gump would declare, "That's all I'm going to say about that!" ('Cuz if I said any more, there would probably be a gazillion little undersize trout swimming around all over the Southeast Louisiana marsh pulling more balloons behind them than you'd need for a neighborhood birthday party at McDonald's!)

Fable 26—if you salt down your bait shrimp, they'll stay on the hook better. Oh, they'll stay on the hook better, but you won't catch anything but hardheads on them. You talk about nasty shrimp! This is another one of those worn-out fishing tips that dates back to the days of the depression, shadrigs, and 60-pound-test braided rayon line. Nobody believes this anymore, y'all.

Fable 27—if you get stuck by a catfish, rub the catfish's own slime on your wound to immediately stop the pain. That's another one of those garlic-totin', WD-40-sprayin', anise-massaging old-timers' stories, concocted by a Falstaff-guzzlin' fisherman back in the heyday of Irish Bayou who actually believed that! Personally, I find that if and when a hardhead stings you, nothing relieves the pain better than a string of genuine,

Naval-approved profanities as long as the deck on an aircraft carrier, combined of course with one of those little crushable ammonia ampules. Trying to rub the fish's own slime on the sting will probably only serve to get you stung a second time! Don't be a dummy—leave the little critter alone.

Fable 28—if a stingray sticks, you submerge the wound in very hot water right away to eliminate the pain. According to the St. Bernard Parish EMTs, that is absolutely correct! The American Medical Association and all of its trauma physicians from Pensacola to Fort Walton Beach to Destin confirmed that ice really doesn't alleviate stingray pain all that much, even though it does serve to localize the venom in a real pinch. What they learned years ago in Florida, where stingray injuries are commonplace, is that hot water virtually neutralizes the effect of the venom and eradicates the pain while you're on your way to medical treatment. So where do you get hot water from on a fishing boat? Out of that little "pee hole" coming from the water pump on the outboard, that's where! Oh, speaking of pee, the story everyone remembers from the TV show "Survivor" is that peeing on a sea-urchin sting relieves the intense burning pain. But that was for sea urchin, y'all. Don't let your fishing buddy talk you into this treatment for stingray punctures! Whoever came up with this fable really went off the wall big time. That or he's having flashbacks from medication he took at Woodstock.

Fable 29—within the very same species there are two kinds of fish—those that bite and those that never bite! Wait—I heard my ol' buddy Capt. Phil Robichaux preaching that philosophy once at a seminar. Do this—remember it, and the next time you guys see each other, you'll have something in common to talk about! I guess the real story about this fable is, yes, there are fish that feed and fish that don't feed. The ones that feed are called "alive." The ones that don't feed are called "dead."

So, uh, how many fables did I forget?

Index

Win a FREE FISHING TRIP with Louisiana's favorite outdoorsman,

FRANK DAVIS!

Go fishing with Frank and get the inside scoop on the best fishing holes in South Louisiana, plus Frank's best fishing tips and advice.

What you need to do:

Fill out and return this form to register to win a free fishing trip for TWO! The winner will be selected by a drawing on July 30, 2004. Trip details to be determined later.

PLEASE PRINT CLEARLY

Name _____

Address _____ City _____ State _____ Zip _____

Phone _____ E-mail _____

Entries must be received before July 30, 2004

Return entries to
Pelican Publishing Company
Attn: Frank Davis Contest
PO Box 3110 * Gretna, LA 70054-3110